EMPLOYMENT OF SPECIAL FORCES:

CHALLENGES AND OPPORTUNITIES FOR THE FUTURE

EMPLOYMENT OF SPECIAL FORCES:

CHALLENGES AND OPPORTUNITIES FOR THE FUTURE

Editor
Col V S Yadav

(Senior Fellow, Centre for Joint Warfare Studies)

Published in association with
Centre For Joint Warfare Studies (CENJOWS)
Kashmir House, Rajaji Marg, New Delhi

Vij Books India Pvt Ltd
Ansari Road, New Delhi (India)

Published by

Vij Books India Pvt Ltd
(Publishers, Distributors & Importers)
2/19, Ansari Road, Darya Ganj
New Delhi - 110002
Phones: 91-11-43596460, 91-11- 65449971
Fax: 91-11-47340674
www.vijbooks.com
e-mail : vijbooks@rediffmail.com

ISBN: 978-93-81411-28-5

Contents

THIRD SESSION

FOURTH SESSION

Approach Paper

The task of SF is proxy application of Force at low and precisely calculated levels, the objective being to achieve some political effect, not a battlefield victory.

Stephen Cohen in 'The Idea of Pakistan'

Introduction

The hostage rescue operation at Entebbe in July 1976 is hailed as one of the most successful integrated special operations in modern, post World War II history. In stark contrast to the Entebbe Operation, the attempted rescue of American hostages from Tehran, in April 1980, was a dismal failure. Deficiencies in mission planning, absence of coordination between individual components and lack of interoperability are often cited as major causes, which led to the debacle. In October 1983, US Special Forces carried out 'Operation Urgent Fury' in Grenada. Though military objectives were achieved, it is remembered more because of the inept planning, leading to lack of coordination in almost every aspect of the operation. It is often said that lessons learnt during the Grenada Operation led to the reorganisation of US Special Forces and the creation of the integrated USSOCOM (United States Special Operations Command).

The 26 November 2008 attack at Mumbai and the subsequent operations to flush out the terrorists brought Indian Special Forces (SF) into sharp focus. The National Security Guard (NSG) component, involved in the operation, mainly comprised personnel on deputation from the Indian Army. The attack itself was audacious and even though it was a suicide mission, it succeeded in achieving the objectives, set by the perpetrators. More recently, in June-July 2010, the orchestration of widespread stone pelting incidents in the Kashmir valley also points towards the likelihood of a well crafted Special Operation, albeit of a very different nature, but one which appeared to be aimed at exploiting dissidence to cause the desired strategic effect. In the prevailing era of strategic uncertainty, carefully structured Special Forces provide a reliable option for application of military force to achieve national security objectives.

Special Forces and Special Operations offer an option for providing an asymmetric response across the entire spectrum of conflict. An asymmetric response does not automatically imply a physical attack; in most cases, direct action should be only the extreme response. Special Forces are meant to achieve strategic objectives through application of modest resources in a calibrated manner.

Special Operations differ from conventional operations with respect to the level of objectives, dividends that accrue in comparison to the force employed, degree of risks (material and political), employment techniques and execution methods. Special Operations, especially at the strategic level, need support and coordination of various agencies, departments and Ministries; detailed operational intelligence being a prime requirement.

While it is universally accepted that SF should rely on individual skills and work in small teams, while operating in joint operations scenarios, assets need to be optimised. SF may be used against a wide range of adversaries, including terrorists, insurgents, guerrillas, or regular combatants.

Objective of the Seminar

A considerable amount of time is spent in developing strategies to address various challenges and threats that lie ahead; which is rightly so. However, there is also a need to focus on opportunities that may emerge and developing the means for exploiting these opportunities.

With an eye on the future, the Seminar is aimed at examining various alternatives for optimal employment of Indian SF, in pursuit of national security goals with a proactive mindset. Concepts, doctrines, organisation structure, training and HR policies would form an integral part of any blue print for the future.

Deliberations during the Seminar are expected to provide valuable inputs from acclaimed professionals and thinkers of different hues and backgrounds, both, from within India and abroad.

SF of India

The Special Forces of India are Indian military units that are trained in special operations. The biggest component of SF is fielded by the Indian Army, but other Services too have SF of varying capabilities catering to their specific needs. In some States, select police units have also been designated as commandos; to be utilised for state specific requirements. All the Special Forces have different tasks, ranging from counter-insurgency to anti-hijacking to guerrilla warfare and focus on individual Service specific requirements.

SF of Foreign Countries

Most professional militaries in the world have raised special units with focussed capabilities, catering for specialised requirements. With the advent of the threat of terrorism and internal strife, Counter Insurgency (CI) and Counter Terrorism (CT) roles have also been added subsequently. In contrast to the Indian situation, the approach to employment of SF is interventionist in nature. Similarly, in some countries, SF are developed more with a role/ mission perspective rather than a geographical area perspective. Literature on foreign SF, particularly Western SF, lists nine core tasks, which are widely adopted with slight variations as per local environments. These tasks are:-

➤ Direct Action.

➤ Strategic Reconnaissance (in hostile territory to include Tech/ Humint).

➤ Foreign Internal Defence (FID) - protect host nation from external/ internal threats, security of the population in host country.

➤ Unconventional Warfare support to resistance organisations as part of the overall effort.

➤ Counter Terrorism (CT).

➤ Counter Proliferation of WMD including securing WMD material/ sites.

➤ Civil Affairs (CA) transition from military to civil governance.

➤   Psychological Operations.

➤   Information Operations.

India is placed in a situation where it has to employ its SF within or very close to its borders. Considering its pre-eminence in the region and the security problems of its neighbours, a situation may develop where India is constrained to intervene in the geo-strategic neighbourhood.

Future Imperatives in the Subcontinent

India's neighbourhood is no longer its 'backyard' as was considered to be earlier. India and Pakistan being nuclear neighbours, in case of a conflict, the rest of the world is certain to exert diplomatic pressure to prevent escalation of the conflict. Thus India is unlikely to have the flexibility to respond to provocative acts by adversaries, with its conventional might. In keeping with its position, astride the Indian Ocean and the SLOC, perhaps the future points towards the need to develop a composite SF capability across the three mediums and across the entire spectrum of conflict, including the capability for roles and tasks of a strategic nature.

The threat of warfare featuring conventional forces may have declined; however, it remains a distinct possibility. While it must still be regarded as the most dangerous threat, few countries in the immediate vicinity are capable of matching India's conventional military combat power. Due to India's conventional superiority, adversaries are more likely to seek indirect forms of conflict. The present trends point towards a shift in the character and forms of future warfare.

Need to Evolve and Improve. Most analysts agree that sub-conventional operations are likely to be the norm in the future, wherein the SF is likely to play an important role. While the capability to complement traditional forces in war is time tested, the SF would need to acquire new skills and develop new tactics, not only to meet likely threats but also to exploit opportunities in a proactive manner. With the strategic focus of India not being confined only to South Asia, language capability and regional and cultural orientation for the SF may also become important. The requirement to continuously evolve and improve Indian SF capability cannot be over emphasised.

State of the Art Equipment

Employment of Indian SF during the terrorist attack at Mumbai, in Nov 2008, highlighted the importance of right equipment for SF missions in an urban scenario. *State of the art* weapons and equipment is one of the important attributes of an effective SF team. While the equipment to be allocated would be governed by the nature of the mission and notwithstanding that SF teams prefer to travel light, as many as 40 specialised items have been identified for a typical SF soldier. High technology systems and weapons have the potential to provide tactical surprise and leverage which could prove to be critical for the success of a mission.

Posers for the Future

At seminars and also through journals, analysts as well as professionals (who have retired) have often voiced varied opinions about the employment philosophy of SF. Contentious issues that have often been highlighted are reflected below:-

➤ Should SF be employed across the border for developing intelligence sources to plug gaps in intelligence?

➤ Does proliferation of SF lead to dilution in quality? Is there a case for specialisation and rationalisation of roles and tasks?

➤ Special Forces are a strategic asset. Their command and control is based on certain guiding principles, especially so because they can play a crucial role in Out Of Area Contingencies. A suitable organisation structure is essential for coordinating and controlling the component which would form part of the Joint Expeditionary Task Force. Is there a case for reviewing the organisation of Indian Special?

➤ Is there a tendency to give more weightage to Direct Action missions over other important SF tasks?

➤ What should be the focus for modernising Special Forces of a developing country like India?

Conclusion

In an era of more 'conflicts' and fewer 'wars', the freedom to employ conventional forces is bound to be restricted. A nation cannot forfeit its responsibility to act decisively even though it would be under increasing constraints. SF offers the option for an effective response which would not be considered as a prelude to war. In highly sensitive ambiguous situations, SF could be the instruments of choice.

Employment of SF for strategic tasks would warrant synergised employment; vertically integrated and centrally controlled, with support from the highest level of the Government.

A debate about future concepts for employment of Special Forces would further lead to the crystallisation of other related issues. Mutual exchange of experiences and ideas between friendly countries should form the cornerstone of any strategy for arriving at the right combination for the future.

SEMINAR

EMPLOYMENT OF SPECIAL FORCES: CHALLENGES AND OPPORTUNITIES FOR THE FUTURE

INAUGURAL SESSION

Opening Remarks	Maj Gen (Retd) KB Kapoor, VSM, Director, CENJOWS
Address	Vice Admiral DK Joshi, PVSM,AVSM, YSM, NM,VSM, Chief Of Integrated Defence Staff to Chairman COSC(CISC), HQ Integrated Defence Staff
Key Note Address	Air Chief Marshal PV Naik,PVSM,VSM,ADC, Chairman, Chief Of Staff Committee and Chief of Air Staff
Vote of Thanks	Shri Jayant Baranwal, CMD , SP Guide Publications

OPENING REMARKS

MAJOR GENERAL(RETD) KB KAPOOR,VSM

Air Chief Marshal PV Naik, Chairman, Chiefs of Staff Committee (COSC) and Chief of Air Staff, Vice Admiral VK Joshi, Chief of Integrated Staff to Chairman Chiefs of Staff Committee (CISC), Headquarter Integrated Defence Staff (HQ IDS), Lt Gen AS Lamba, Vice Chief of Army Staff, Gen Kalkat, Mr Baranwal, CMD of SP Guide Publications, eminent panelists, senior officers, both serving and retired from the Army, officers from the defence services, members of media- Ladies and gentlemen. I welcome you all to this seminar on "Employment of Special Forces, Challenges and Opportunities for the Future". This seminar is being jointly organised by Headquarter IDS, SP Guide Publications and Centre for Joint Warfare Studies. We are honoured by the presence of the Chairman, Chiefs of Staff Committee, who guides and oversees the evolution and employment of Special Forces (SF) in defence services also by the distinguished members of the fraternity forces from home and abroad.

History is replete with examples of actions carried out by small teams of Special Forces which have changed not only the course of operations but also of the war. These men with extra-ordinary courage, dedication, abundant initiative, indomitable spirit and with scant respect to their personal safety have achieved results where conventional forces could not be employed. Some of these actions have been documented while a lot of them remained shrouded in mystery because of political and security reasons. Special Forces have been used from time immemorial; some of the examples are specialised units of Hamilcar Barsca of Sicily. Specialised units of Knight Templars in

Crusade wars, Ninjas of China and Japan, even the employment of such forces also find mention in the Indian military writings of Kautiliya. But it is in the latter half of the 20th century that Special Forces have come into higher prominence.

Governments discovered that objectives can sometimes be achieved by small teams of anonymous specialists than a larger, much more politically controversial conventional deployment, the most recent examples of these being, Kosovo and Afghanistan. The future wars are going to be fought in the spectrum encompassing from nuclear, conventional, sub-conventional as also in the domains of land, sea, undersea, air, space and even cyber space. The success against a superior and evenly matched adversary will be achieved by creating asymmetry. This is the space where the task of Special Forces would emerge. Their mission, thus, lies in geo-strategic, strategic operations or tactical level and may be politico-military in nature like the ill-fated raid of British commandos in Libya last week.

The era has also witnessed the mushrooming of Special Forces like Green Berets, Special Operation Group, Naval Seals, SAS etc. In India too, we had a similar trend of raising Parachute Commandos, Marcos, Garuds of Defence Services, and Special Action Groups of NSG, Cobra of Andhra Pradesh and a host of others, under the Centre and State police forces. In all the wars India has fought, these forces have merely been used at the tactical level. At times, mathematical distribution of Special Forces is done at the tactical level. More recently, only limited employment of these forces has been seen in low intensity conflict and insurgency. Do these highly trained and motivated units have a role at geo-strategic level both in war and peace? As the emerging regional power, we have to look at our area of interest from Straits of Hormuz to Straits of Malacca. Do we have a defined role for our forces or such forces in our area of interest? Also, who should plan their employment, their training, their equipping and career progression? These are some of issues that we would deliberate in the next two days and I am sanguine that our panelists with their experience, would enlighten us and show us the way ahead.

The proceedings of the seminar along with the recommendations of Centre for Joint Warfare Studies will be one of the inputs to Headquarter

Integrated Defence Staff for the evolution of a doctrine on employment of Special Forces, which on finalisation, will be put up to Chairman, Chiefs of Staff Committee who is present with us today. With these words I will now request Admiral DK Joshi, CISC, Headquarter IDS, to address the Seminar.

ADDRESS

VICE ADMIRAL DK JOSHI, PVSM, AVSM, YSM, NM, VSM

Chairman, Chiefs of Staff Committee and Chief of Air Staff, Air Chief Marshal, PV Naik, General Lamba, Vice-Chief of Army Staff, General Lidder, erstwhile CISC, General Kalkat, Director Emeritus CENJOWS, invitees from friendly foreign countries, distinguished guests, ladies and gentlemen. At the outset I would like to extend a very warm welcome to each one of you and in particular convey our sincere thanks to Chairman, COSC for having accepted our invitation to deliver the Key Note Address at the inaugural session of this seminar. Amongst eminent panelists for the seminar, we have speakers from Israel, France, Germany and the former head and Colonel Commandant of the famed SAS from UK. The rich experience accumulated under difficult combat conditions should provide us with considerable food for thought. I am sure that participants look forward to their presentations with a great deal of anticipation.

History is replete with the examples of spectacular and successful missions undertaken by Special Forces which have often turned the tide in a war. While there is a need to retain core competencies and individualities of services or arms, as in every other form of warfare, in special operations too, there is an overriding requirement of interoperability and jointness without which success would be difficult to come by. Lack of coordination between individual components has often been cited as an impediment to achieving desired outcomes from a SF Mission. I am sure, that the participants will address these issues in sufficient depth and at appropriate levels. In the November 2008 operation in Mumbai, to weed out terrorists, SF operations again came into sharp focus. Though, it was essentially a counter terrorism operation, the importance of correct equipment and training, while operating in an urban setting, was highlighted in ample measure. I am confident that with the participation from the industry in this seminar we should be able to take forward the process of identifying evolving technologies, suitable to the Indian context.

In trying to conceive a vision for Special Forces, we realise that there are many factors which are inter-twined, ranging from policy and national security interests at the macro level to an effective command and control organisation at the execution level. Equipping and training Special Forces requires an efficient supporting organisational structure that is vibrant and stays ahead of the game. The special operations command architectures of different countries would certainly be a model to be examined so as to arrive at a structure of Special Forces that suits us best. Experts would debate such issues over the next two days and arrive at a way ahead in the concluding session. More than anything else, I believe, it is the fleet footedness, agility, the ability to think quickly on their feet and innovate, to adapt rapidly to dynamic situations that sets apart a successful SF operation from an embarrassment. It will seldom happen that local support, background intelligence and complete knowledge of a rapidly evolving situation are available in an ideal manner.

SF operatives will constantly need to cultivate a mindset to succeed against overwhelming odds. To illustrate this mindset that I am talking about, I can do no better than recite a few lines from Pandit Ram Prasad Bismil's poem "*Sarfaroshi Ki Tamanna*". Those of you who saw the movie Rang De Basanti would readily recall these lines. *Haath jin main ho junoon kat te nahi talwar se, sur jo uth jate hain wo jhukte nahi lalkaar se, aur bhadkega jo shola sa hamare man main hai, sarfaroshi ki tamanna ab hamare dil main hai"*. This junoon or the fanatical kind of mindset, I believe, is a critical requirement apart from training, equipping and preparedness as the key to successful SF operations. To borrow from Shakespeare's *Julius Caesar*, "Yond Cassius has a lean and hungry look.   He thinks too much. Such men are dangerous". To my mind, SF operatives have to be lean and hungry, not in the physical sense but in the sense of craving for successful operations against overwhelming odds. They have to be thinking men. They have to be dangerous men. With these gentlemen, I request Chairman COSC to deliver his keynote address.

KEY NOTE ADDRESS

AIR CHIEF MARSHAL PV NAIK, PVSM, VSM, ADC

Vice Admiral Joshi, General Kalkat, General Kapoor, Shri Jayant Baranwal, distinguished guests in the audience from India and abroad. From my physique, I am sure; all of you have understood that I am not a Special Forces man. Once upon a time I could have been but not now. Well, all the same, it is a pleasure to be amongst you and be amongst the acclaimed strategists and extremely experienced professionals to deliberate upon a subject which has a growing significance in today's evolving security scenario. It is certainly not about licence to kill but more about capability to enforce the will and I will come back to this a little later.

The realities in today's world are much more threatening as compared to the glamorous fiction of 007 James Bond and his heart in the mouth antics. Commandos laddering down to the roof top at Nariman Point or SAS evacuating their citizens are more frequent today as is the evolution of the Bonds into their new avatar. So what is it that makes all of us talk so much about Special Forces operations more today than say yesterday or the day before? Structured military activities have always required the support of specialised assets in order to achieve their objectives. Hence, Special Forces have gained in prominence over the years. It has been found that certain objectives can easily be achieved, like it was brought out by the speakers before me, by a small team of specialists than a larger and much more politically controversial deployment. Carved out from the regular armed forces cadre or security forces, Special Forces are high value assets and this is one point that we need to keep in mind, throughout, highly capable of delivering effects, disproportionate to their size. If you look at today's, what I call fourth generation warfare, it basically encompasses, attempts to circumvent or undermine the enemy's strengths while exploiting his weaknesses. This warfare thrives on using methods that differ substantially from the opponent's usual modus-operandi. Now throughout their evolution during the 20th and 21st century, the Special Forces units have had many spectacular successes in achieving national objectives also. No wonder that the mention of Special Forces certainly fills us with a bit of overwhelming kind of awe and respect for these brave men. Legends abound about having six drinks and thereafter eating the glass tumbler and then running 25 miles to capture an objective. All of us have heard these legends. Some of them are true.

In today's era of fierce wars and intense conflicts, sub-conventional threats assume greater significance. Neutralising threats across the entire spectrum of conflicts, poses challenges which are quantitatively and qualitatively different. Hence, ladies and gentlemen, we need to cater to a full spectrum of threats from nuclear confrontation, through conventional war to conflicts limited in area, scope or objectives. We need, therefore, a full range of capabilities with the ability to dynamically swing between them. Future conflicts, as I am sure all of you will agree, are likely to be swift, sharp, intense as well as more challenging and more unpredictable. They will require a capability for assured calibrated and flexible responses as well as a projection of national power in all forms. Being a combat aviator, I understand the pivotal position that Special Forces occupy in the prosecution of military operations and I am aware that these are the forces that can be surgically employed in conflict scenarios to achieve your aims. The fact that a lot of nations are downsizing their armed forces and adding muscle to their Special Forces, says it all.

There is much to learn from the experience of special operations across the world be it Iran, Iraq and now Afghanistan, which have demonstrated the increasing employability and viability of Special Forces. All successful and some not so successful missions like Entebbe, Mogadishu, the Iranian Embassy seize etc, need political and military backing for success of any kind. The current Libyan crisis where British and German Special Forces came for specialised operations and evacuation of their citizens, has reiterated the fact that Special Forces are going to be the x-factor for achieving national objectives. Obviously why India should be left behind? Well all of us understand that Special Forces can be employed for strategic, operational as well as tactical roles. We are also aware that SF operations include a multitude of operations inclusive of suppression of enemy air defence (SEAD), counter air, close air support etc. What is important is understanding their high value significance. The fact is that SF operations are intrinsically joint but different from conventional forces. And that they are not really a substitute for conventional forces, be it unconventional warfare, counter-terrorism, psy-ops or counter proliferation, roles are plenty. But for each role, Special Forces will always be dependent on detailed intelligence, intimate and responsive command and control as they have the ability to by-pass all sea or land objectives. The planning also has to cater for mobility, counter-mobility, survivability, fire support, communications, link-ups etc. And hence, planning is as important as the execution.

In today's warfare where there is a blur between war and politics, soldiers and civilian targets, peace and conflict, battle field or fratricide, there is a big challenge in SF operations. Additional challenges include integration with conventional forces as well as government agencies, when needed. However, in all this, the Special Forces must preserve their autonomy to protect and encourage the unconventional approach, which is the soul of SF. On the part of powers that be, there is an inability, I feel, to conceptualise the application of special operations theory and doctrines, especially in our context. Added to it, there is an inexplicable reluctance on the part of our military to forge an integrated joint services approach towards the SF and special operations. All this is because, in my opinion, even the military poorly understands SF capabilities and they see the SF as the shadow guys, who go and fight their own war. While I do not wish to dwell on aspects that are best left to experts, I do hope the seminar examines the issue of concept of employment of Special Forces in its entirety, during the next couple of days.

In India we have ten thousand plus Special Forces. They are scattered, service specific or domain specialised. The question is do we have a national vision or policy for the employment and the risk taking of these forces? As you know, there is political fallout for the kind of missions undertaken by Special Forces. Now, while political will can change overnight, the capability cannot be built overnight. In the current scenario when sometimes adversaries dictate the rules of engagements, we require to act swiftly, flexibly and decisively. The reaction time would ultimately decide the outcome of a mission. In crisis situations, Special Forces could create the much needed headways in unpredictable ways and enable conventional forces to regroup, plan and strike. Therefore, a quicker reaction time would mean that we pack some essentials into this tight knitted entity. The Special Forces must have a flatter command and structure, high mobility, flexibility in thought and action, sound intelligence, communications back-up, technological superiority and the biggest advantage of all secrecy and security, both during peace and war. These vital constituents make these forces adaptable, lethal units, capable of achieving limited objectives and what is important is thereby opening a large number of options to the national leadership. In times of crisis like the 26/11 incident in Mumbai, what the leadership needed were options. So Special Forces could create many more options for the national leadership in times of National crisis. It is important that first we clearly identify the roles for missions within our sphere of operations; deliberations during the seminar should provide you with good pointers in this direction. Thank you and Jai Hind.

VOTE OF THANKS

MR JAYANT BARANWAL

Air Chief Marshal PV Naik, Chairman, Chiefs of Staff Committee and Chief of Air Staff, Vice Admiral VK Joshi, CISC Headquarter IDS, Lt Gen AS Lamba, Vice Chief of Army Staff, Gen Kalkat, Gen Kapoor, Director CENJOWS, eminent panelists, officers from the defence services, members of media, ladies and gentlemen. On behalf of SP Guide Publications and CENJOWS, I wish to thank all of you to have come here to attend this seminar on Special Forces. As you are all aware, there is a need for a well laid down national level policy for this vital element of security of our nation, i.e. Special Forces. We at SP Guide Publications remain committed with our intentions to do everything to complement the cause of security and defence of our country. Joining hands with CENJOWS, is a reflection of our humble attempt to reflect our intentions. We are honoured by the presence of Chief of Air Staff and thank him for taking time out of his very busy schedule. We are grateful to our panelists from abroad, who could take time out to share their views. The panelists are distinguished speakers of Special Forces who would share their experiences and views with us. Thanks to Vice Admiral Joshi, CISC. And we express our thanks to Lt Gen(Retd) AS Kalkat, Director Emeritus, CENJOWS.

CONCEPT OF EMPLOYMENT OF FOREIGN SPECIAL FORCES

SECOND SESSION

Chairperson   Lt Gen (Retd) HS Lidder

Speakers

Employment of Special Forces: Lt Gen (Retd) Sir Graeme Lamb,
United Kingdom   Former Colonel Commandant SAS,
                                    United Kingdom

Employment of Special Forces: Brigadier General Eyal Eizenberg,
Israel   Israel Defence Forces

Employment of Special Forces: Col Philippe Landicheff, French Air
France   Force, French Special Operations
                                    Command

Employment of Special Forces: Brigadier General (Retd) Hans
Germany   Christoff Ammon, Former Commander
                                    German Army Special Forces

Discussion

BIO DATA OF PANELISTS

Chairperson

Lt Gen (Retd) HS Lidder, PVSM, UYSM, YSM, VSM, ADC, former Chief of Integrated Defence Staff to the Chairman, Chief of Staff Committee (CISC), Headquarter Integrated Defence Staff. A Commando Dagger, he has served in 3 Para, 9 Para Special Forces, 10 Para Special Forces and commanded 9 Para Special Forces with distinction in Operation Pawan.

He has been an Instructor in Commando School, Belgaum and Senior Command Wing, Army War College, Mhow. The General has held a number of important staff appointments, including Brigade Major of a Mountain Brigade, General Staff Officer in Military Operations Directorate at Army Headquarters, Colonel (Combat Power) in Headquarters Army Training Command, Colonel General Staff (Operations) in a Command Headquarters, Deputy Director General of Perspective Planning (Strategy) at Army Headquarters and Chief of Staff in Headquarters Army Training Command. He was the first military liaison officer in Embassy of India at Colombo during Operation Pawan.

He has been Defence Advisor in Embassy of India in Washington for over three years. The General has extensive experience of sub-conventional warfare, having commanded a Brigade along Line of Control in Mendhar District (Jammu & Kashmir), a Rashtriya Rifles Force in Rajouri District (Jammu & Kashmir) and a Corps combating counter insurgency in the North Eastern States of Assam and Arunachal Pradesh. He assumed the appointment of Chief of Integrated Defence Staff to the Chairman Chief of Staff Committee on 03 Mar 2006 and hung his uniform on 01 October 2008.

Speakers

Lt Gen (Retd) Sir Graeme Lamb, KBE, CMG, DSO, former head of SAS and Commander of the British Field Army. Commissioned into the Queen's own High Landers, he has served in numerous staff and operational appointments including Commanding the 5th Airborne Brigade, the 3rd Division, various doctrines and training posts and as Assistant Commandant at the staff of the Joint Services Command and Staff College. He completed UKSF selection in 1977 and an extended Troop Commanders tour of duty, returning as a Squadron Commander as a result of the Falklands Campaign. On completion of his Staff College Course, he returned as the Operations Officer and again as a Lieutenant Colonel, Special Forces, in direct support of Lieutenant General Sir Peter De La Billiere for the 1st Gulf War. He was selected as Director Special Forces in March 2001, where he has overseen global operations, specifically the Balkans, Afghanistan and Iraq. He stepped down as Commander of the Field Army in July 2009 and returned to Afghanistan at the direct request of General David Petraeus and General Stanley McChrystal, of the US Army to scope a programme designed to repeat the success in Iraq whereby insurgents are persuaded to give up their arms.

Brigadier General Eyal Eizenberg, Commander Gaza Division, Israel Defence Forces. Conscripted to the IDF from 1981 – 1989, initially as a cadet in the Israeli Air-Force Flight School. Then, joined the Shaldag Unit. From 1990 to 1991, he commanded the Samson's Foxes Reconnaissance Company. From 1993 to 1995, he was the Commander of the Shaked Infantry Battalion. From 1995-96, he was the head of Operations Branch, Air Force Special Forces Command. From 1996 to 1999, he commanded the Shaldag Unit, the Air-Force Special Forces.

He has also commanded the Israeli withdrawal from the security zone in Southern Lebanon. As Commander, Reserve Paratrooper Brigade from 2001–2003, he commanded it during Operation Defensive Shield. From 2003 – 2005, as Commander of Givati Brigade, he led the Brigade during Operation Days of Penitence. He was a Commander of the paratrooper division from 2005-2008. As the Commander of Gaza Division, from 2008-2010, he has lead the Cast Lead operation.

Colonel Landicheff Philippe, French Air Force. He was commissioned as Nuclear Security Officer in the year 1989. In 1991, he attended the Commando Parachutist N°10 in Nimes, as J3 Chief. Promoted as Captain in August 1992, he participated in missions in Saudi Arabia and in Bosnia. And in 1995 he was commissioned as Instructor at the Air Academy in Salon. In 1997, promoted as Major, he took the command of the CPA 10 in APT, the only Air commando unit dedicated to FR SOCOM. He participated in missions with CJSOTF in Bosnia.

After one year at the War College in PARIS, in 2003, he took command of the CPA 30 in Bordeaux which is dedicated to CSAR Mission. He participated in the OEF mission in Afghanistan, in 2004. In 2007, at French SOCOM Headquarters, he lead the International Relationship Division for all kinds of cooperation that French SOCOM can have. He has been awarded the Legion of Honour, National Order of Merit (Officer) and Military Valour Cross, with one unit citation.

Brigadier General (Retd) Hans Christoph Ammon, former Commander German Army Special Forces. He originally joined the German Bundeswehr in 1970, for a period of two years and was stationed with Armoured Artillery Batallion 75. General Ammon attended the 24th General Staff Officers Course at the Bundeswehr Command and General Staff College and also the 42nd Staff Course at the Defence Services Staff College in Wellington, India. In October 1989, General Ammon was posted as Commanding Officer to

Armoured Artillery Batallion 25.

In the year 1994, he had his first operational deployment as Chief of Staff of the German Contingent, United Nations Somalia Mission (UNOSOM II). In January 1997, General Ammon arrived in HQ Allied Rapid Reaction Corps (ARRC) to take up the appointment as ACOS G3. During this time he deployed with HQ ARRC in 1999, for eight months, to Macedonia and Kosovo in order to command as HQ KFOR, the initial entry operation of NATO Forces into Kosovo.

One of his very important postings was when General Ammon was posted to the German Ministry of Defence as Chief Operations Planning at Armed Forces Staff, while he was particularly responsible for the Joined Planning of German contribution to Operation Enduring Freedom and ISAF. In September 2003, he was appointed Commander of Mechanised Infantry Brigade 30. During this time he deployed with his Brigade in Afghanistan, in 2005. In July 2007, General Ammon was appointed Commander, German Army Special Forces. He held his command until September, 2010 when he finished his military career. General Ammon has been awarded the order of merit of the Federal Republic of Germany, Operations Medal KVM and KFOR and Medaille de la Defence Nationale(FRA).

OPENING REMARKS

Lt Gen (Retd) HS Lidder, PVSM, UYSM, YSM, VSM, ADC

We commence this session which deals with the concept of employment of foreign Special Forces. As you can see we have a very eminent panel with us. It spans the SF activity from UK to France to Israel and Germany. These countries have long been practitioners of Special Forces and have huge amount of experience to share with us and I am sure at the end of their presentations, you will be able to identify those information gaps which you would like to be filled in and I would like you to please feel free to ask questions. Speakers have been asked to cover the concept of employment and roles assigned to their Special Forces, the organisational structure at the macro level and human resources policies, intra-operability aspects, exploiting core competency of individual service components, analysis of major missions and tasks, strengths and weak areas. The weightage is assigned to direct action missions in planning, training and equipping of Special Forces and future strategies in the emerging geo-strategic environment vis-à-vis the country involved. I first request Gen Lamb to kindly come and make his presentations. We will take questions in the end, gentlemen.

Employment of Special Forces : United Kindgom

Lt Gen (Retd) Sir Graeme Lamb

During the inaugural session, Vice Admiral Joshi and other speakers had mentioned that there was a need to have Special Forces who were adaptable, who were courageous, who were thinkers and who were lean and hungry. They omitted to mention that what was really important was, they all have wickedly good looks. Now, I never really follow this script on anything I have ever done when I was serving or now that I am retired but I have run broadly through the questions that were asked in addressing this morning's discussion.

I think what is really important is that we understand the context sub-nationally, nationally, regionally and internationally, that you will find yourselves operating in what is a very different century, unlike all those that have gone before us. I believe that there has been a significant paradigm shift, not well recognized, not well understood, that is occurring and has occurred as we came out of the 20th century and now find ourselves in the 21st and let me tell you why. I think all those maxims ie find, fix and strike, have been completely turned on their heads. I remember when I first went to Germany as a young officer, looking across the inner German border, what was then the principal threat of the Soviet Union; we had very small find capabilities. We had elements of force which were there to fix the large strike, manoeuvre forces, whether they were on the Atlantic and the gap, whether they were over Poland, Germany and into Russia, for the to and fro, for the air or whether it was on the ground forces. I would suggest that in this century, the paradigm shift has completely reversed. The problem we now face in the 21st century is, how to find and fix, which is inherently more complicated. It is not about a large force from which you manoeuvre around. But it is the use of money, diplomacy, politics, economics, capitalism, you name it, it is all those being brought to bear this fix. Those who would threaten us and strike, have moved into that which is no longer about just precision. In my view, precision strike on steroids, where you have to be very very accurate in what you strike.

Industrial violence is no longer the monopoly of the Nation state. It was these last centuries, you know the old British Empire, we had a huge navy, we could deploy forces to bring industrial level violence to bear and you needed that underpinned by the western model of the Nation state. In this century, industrial violence is no longer that monopoly. Because only a few people and I could probably pick a few, out of any single of the rows here, can bring industrial violence to bear on a Nation State, whether that is chemical, biological, radiological or nuclear. We have been fixated by weapons of mass destruction as we came out of the last century and into the new and rightly so because they represent a very clear and present danger. I went to Tokyo in 1994, that's 17 years ago, to see the Aum Sect who had just gassed the underground, killed 15 and hospitalized five and half thousand people because they have been able to produce weapons grade Sarin, Nerve Gas. They were dabbling in biological weapons. They just hadn't employed it properly, although they had the wherewithal to do it. If they used the dispersion methods they had available, they would have killed near about 5 thousand or more of their own people and they were lunatics who tied themselves to low voltage but had 60 million dollars of disposable capital in order to create that capability. Industrial violence in this century can be brought to bear on your Nation State, on its people, on your way of life, and your prosperity by just a few. That is a harsh fact. The power of one can be brought to bear on your screens by the suicide bomber. And he brings fear across your population. His method is quite simple. The means, by which he projects that terror is through the media, is through mass communication, just as we see in Tunisia, in Libya, in Egypt, Yemen, anywhere else, in London. It can be brought to bear any moment and since, it becomes close and personal to the individual, to everyone of your member, whether it be India, whether it be United Kingdom whether it be America, they communicate that fear and terror.

The power of the individual, his 15 minutes worth of fame, now becomes something which is very clear because all through this last century we had the three obvious commons, Land, Air and Sea, to deal with. We have today, the problem of dealing with Air, Land, Sea and what I would roughly call communication space and that includes space, cyber, media, communications etc. The ability to be twittering, to be blogging through the internet, to be able to energize, whether it is benevolently or malevolently, huge energies amongst people who are disaffected, angry, is absolutely omnipresent. Clare Lockhart wrote a very good book which is called "Failed and Failing States". It is her assessment that by 2020-2025, there will be, somewhere in the region of 40-70 failed or failing states on the globe. Now you can work out the mathematics and the Indian Army, Navy and Air Force are enormous bodies. But you would run out of people at about failed state 3 or 4. We just don't have enough people in uniform to be able to contain and on a simple binary basis or control those numbers of people, those numbers of states will absolutely outface. Whether it be NATO, the United Nations, whichever Super Powers, India, China, United States of America care to engage with them. We know from our experience in Iraq and Afghanistan and elsewhere worth in Africa, Sierra Leones and Mogadishus, that these events take up huge numbers of people. So this century, I would suggest gentlemen, is very different and here is the final twist in the tale. We are fixated often politically, militarily, culturally, into seeing because that is how it was projected that the state has been an omnipresent threat. State or non state enterprises should be those which we should be prepared to challenge. That has not gone away. But do not become fixated by it. Because as I look around the world, as I looked through my period of time operating on all the continents and even now when I am in retirement, I sense the threats that are very real. They take all of what I said before, and put it into context, are the trans-national and the sub-national threats, they sit within our countries and are influenced from outside. And if we do not think, how we should address this, then I sense we will not be doing what the Armed Forces of any nation's first responsibility is, which is the defence of their own nation, the defence of its prosperity and the defence of its people. This is the context under which you need lean and hungry men and you need thinking men and women to address the problems that are here already.

If you merely polish the family silver, that which you have had in the past and have done well with, that has helped your nation emerge, progress, survive, then I sense you would not be giving proper and due service to the people who look to the Armed Forces, against the threats that you will face that are already here. People would have been planning yesterday, were planning today and will be planning tomorrow to bring industrial violence to my people in the United Kingdom and I think we should be prepared to do something about it. So my view would be simply this that the individual can manipulate or create, through communication space, public outrage, public disorder, public dissent, public chaos etc. Weapons of mass disorder are probably more worrying than weapons of mass destruction. And secondly, those individuals can challenge and undermine state authority through suicide attacks, fear, creating sectarian and internal sub-national tensions fuelled by trans-national money support or by chemical, biological, radiological or nuclear attack or that of mass destruction. Hopeless situations create the perfect setting for what the hell purpose you get for 15 minutes of fame for those individuals who now have the wherewithal to challenge the state, to challenge your authority and to kill your people, to kill prosperity, to kill hope. Is that not a field of Special Forces, should be applying their thought, mind energy and interest towards rather than polishing the family silver of what either the United Kingdom, Israel, Germany, France, America, or any other nations have been involved in.

Learn from the past but look forward to the future. I think India is in a fascinating place. You have huge new energies besides fiscal, population, education, to be able to move your Armed Forces and your Special Forces to a place that will be more difficult for us more established forces. The question is whether you can do it. So as an organisation, my view will be simply this, you need to reflect on the ability to find, fix and strike, within your Special Forces and a find is about selected human and organisational mapping and analysis, find is about targeted human and organisational tracking and shaping and find is directed human and organisation destruction, both kinetic and non kinetic. You have to understand the forces that are operating against you and they are not clear. You know terror without borders, criminality without frontiers. These are the harsh realities which the Special Forces community should be addressing their minds to, along with the political authority, your inter-agency partners and the Armed Forces is how they support that function in understanding that the prime focus should be on your ability to find those threats which are a clear and present danger to this nation.

Fix is about influence operations, it is about positive intervention. It's going before rather than after the event. We get fixated on our ability to be able to deploy once a situation has unfolded and we have to be able to do that. What is absolutely crucial is your prior energy to be there before it goes wrong, probably the finest operation I conducted as a Special Forces operator was in Macedonia. We could see or we sensed that the third Balkan civil war was about to unfold. So we went and talk to Gen. Smith, we went and talked to George Robertson and we put forces in place with Macedonians, and in this case, with those north from Kosovo, to ensure that a misunderstanding or a misdirected action did not lead to miscalculation and the third civil war erupting. We didn't kill anybody. We got shot at ever so often. We did some arrangement. We made mass communication to make sure that each side understood that they were transgressing and then we did a disarmament programme and we didn't get to the third civil war. So, it wasn't about the body count, it wasn't about the kinetic action. It is in its simplest form; it was about complexity because while these previous centuries have been dangerous and difficult, this one, this one is just hugely more complex.

Fix is about political influence in excess. I sense as I look at India, you have and for a good reason, a relationship between the political authority and your military authority which is separated. I sense it needs to come a little closer. Because when you have sub-national problems, fuelled by trans-national interests, trust me it will go ballistic in a moment and become very political. Mumbai is a good example. Mumbai, you know, Mumbai 2, Mumbai 3, Mumbai 4, this is not, in fact, applied here to India. It will occur, in Europe, Britain, Washington, or else where. Those who would oppose order or the rule, as we know it, they do follow Darwin's very clear advise which is, it is not the strongest of the species which survive but it is those which adapt. And they adapt at a frightening speed. Somebody asked me the other day how will it finish with Libya? I said probably with uncertainty from the regime and uncertainty from the rebels. But understand this, to borrow a line from Sir Winston Churchill "this as it falls out will only be the end of the beginning". We have not begun to understand the complications of what this will bring to us, in a wider sense.

Fix is about shared capabilities with national intelligence agencies. Fix is about shared capabilities with other national Special Forces and their agencies. It's about your relationship inside and outside. People talk about the whole of the Government. What I see often is the 'whole' of the Government and all you have to do is remove the 'W'. The 'hole' is very self evident. Agencies do not cross across. Diplomacy doesn't talk. The foreign office in our case doesn't talk as it should do with the military. The military is not close enough with GCHQ, MI6, MI5 and the rest. Everybody protecting their budget, protecting their selfish self interest and yet you face a single common threat and how those are brought together, is about fixing.

Finally, strike is about precision on steroids. Force interval, still critical and pre-conventional strike capably in these Special Forces, still part. On your strengths and weaknesses, understand this brand equity. Prepare your own self and others for failure, because you will absolutely face it. The assumption that you are always good, that you will always succeed is not how it plays out. You have to manage that with your political authority, with you military authority, with your nation because they will be disappointed ever so often. The mark of a Special Forces soldier, in my view, is his ability to walk away from the situation, not walk into it.

People, people, people, human capital and your investment is the key. You cannot spend enough time, energy and effort and make sure you have the very best thinkers, the very best soldiers as part of that group. And it is about people, it is about purpose and the least important is pay. Direct action versus strategic reconnaissance versus support and influence operations are shaped by strategic influence, framed by strategic reconnaissance and exploited by direct action. Get there, get it sorted and get back capabilities are expensive. The SF are not necessarily a cheap option. Balance of investment, at best it would be 30%- 30% -30%, strategic influence, support in influence, strategic reconnaissance and direct action. And here I guarantee, most people immediately fall to how big is my gun. They look towards direct actions being the pay all and the end all of Special Forces. My view is not that. In fact I would apply probably a balance of 40% on support and influence, 30% on your strategic reconnaissance and 20% on being bloody good at direct action.

You have to have generalists, specialists and experts. The bulk of your Special Forces should be generalists, a few specialists and you do need some experts when you get into some of these technical fields. To the future, it is about shaping and influencing, it is about mapping and tracking. It is about innovation and integration. It is about being lean and hungry and filling your space with thinkers.

Employement of Special Forces : Israel

Brigadier General Eyal Eizenberg

It is a pleasure for me to be here with you. It is my first time in India and I have here three main challenges. First to think I am able to speak in English, the second one is to make you understand my English and the third one is to share with you my small experience. I will speak to you today on the topic of the Special Forces. My presentation is going to focus on the challenges facing us in the future battlefield, definition of Special Forces, its main structures, and how the units are structured. The third point is main activation modes of the Special Forces.

As you can see, in the future we are going to face new challenges within the battlefield. To start with, this is a fight between a nation and a terror organisation which has nation capabilities, for example, Google Earth. In the past, only countries could use UAVs to take pictures of a certain strategic location, today everyone, including terror organisations can get these images very easily by using just Google Earth and the internet. In the past we use to look for the decisive now in these days it is from decisive to attrition. For this reason we need to be patient and to know how to deal with this campaign. The next challenge of course is the technological developments that any terror organisation can use very easily, can buy very easily on the internet; for example, night vision, thermal vision, all this equipment you can buy just on the internet. The next point or the next challenge that rears its head is the new front. The terror organisations understand our weaknesses in the home land security field and they use it. The next challenge is difficulty in singling out and targeting the enemy. The enemy is not a clear entity. And the last one is violating a country's sovereignty by indirect means such as Scud missiles, Fajar rockets etc. Because of these new challenges, the importance of the Special Forces has become essential.

If I try to define Special Forces, they are basically small units, small size units, if you compare them to the regular army, military units, operating to achieve highly strategic targets during peace time and war.

The Operational Model

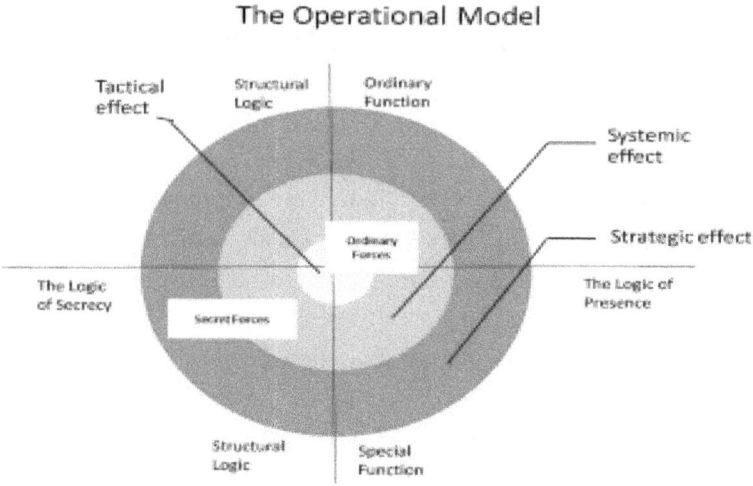

As presented here is the Operational Model, the Armed Forces operate on three main circles. The inner most one is the tactical circle, as you see. The second one is the systemic circle, what you call systemic effect and the third outer most is the strategic circle. The X vertical line is based on presence and secrecy logic as you see and while Y vertical line is based on an ordinary function and special function. According to our understanding, the ordinary forces work mainly in the tactical circle and they have a tactical effect. The secret forces work mainly on the third circle, what you call the strategic circle and they have the strategic effect and the Special Forces can work from the inner circle, from the tactical circle usually in a time up to the systemic circle and even in the strategic circle. For these reasons we need to cooperate with other agencies, for example, in Israel, it is the Mosad and the Shubak.

The Special Forces units are mainly characterised by first of all, clear designation in case of emergency or war. The high quality of human resources that is carefully selected and well trained, have the superior and quality intelligence from all the agencies and they have an ongoing process of learning during the campaign. They have also technological edge and high motivation and high fighting spirit. As I previously mentioned, the Special

Forces can operate in two main situations. The first is in case of emergency or war. The main designation of the Special Forces is to be ready in case of emergency or war. Therefore, they need to be ready for action at all time, 24 hours, 7 days a week. The Special Forces can be used by policy makers in order to achieve national goals. It is another tool in the box. The Special Forces cannot decide a war. They can only complement or support the main manoeuvre. The Special Forces' typical missions in this situation are collecting intelligence, assaulting and damaging enemy ability of C4I, attacking strategic targets and damaging supply routes and there can also be deception effort. In the other operational situation, which we call MOOTW which means Military Operation Other Than War, the forces are activated for some local task other than war. This is an opportunity for the forces to develop and to maintain their ability for cases of emergency or war. Typical missions, in MOOTW are counter-terrorism, intelligence collecting, psychological warfare, operating against proliferation of weapons of mass destruction and humanitarian operations.

This is our general structure in Israel. As you can see, for each branch we have Special Forces, to the Air Force, to the intelligence, to the Navy, to the Ground Forces, they can work together on the same mission and they work alone. They can work in different regional commands or diversely under the general staff. In each of our Special Forces there are, I think, four main branches. First of all, the intelligence is a very big branch. The technological units that support the training, support the trains and maintain the units and of course the operating units itself. I call this the iceberg. Usually what will you see when something is published in the newspaper? Is just what we see above the water, is just as they operate a unit. But under the water there is a doctrine, there is the training, there is a command and control, the equipment and intelligence and the last one, the important one is the human resource. As said earlier, 20% iceberg is above the water, 80% is under the water and this is the Special Forces, actually. It is not just the soldier, it is the headquarters that support the units. This headquarters make those units so unique, so special.

Thank you very much for listening to me and I hope that we all will cooperate in the future as a big Special Forces against the world of terror.

Employement of Special Forces : France

Col Philippe Landicheff

I am Col Landicheff from the French SOCOM. First of all I would like to apologize for my very bad accent. As you can see, I am not your native speaker but I will do my best. I would like to warmly thank Indian Defence Forces and CENJOWS to allow me to express what is the French point of view for the future of the Special Forces. Before going any further, I would like to take the opportunity to present to you what the French Special Forces are.

We have a great original model and to start, I would like to show you a small movie, summing up what we are. So as you were able to see in this small movie, we have a joint system. It's a young structure which has been created in 1992 after the first war in Iraq, for the French. Of course the Special Forces were not born in 1992. We participated in the Second World War in close coordination with SAS. We were embedded in their team. We were taught by the SAS in their forties. And we took into account the example of the US, especially during Eagle Claw Mission in Tehran and after this mission, US decided to create US SOCOM in 1987. We had also learned our lessons. After this war in Iraq, we have marked that we had a lack of coordination of C-II structure to employ at the best level, all these Special Forces, provided by all the service. So we decided to create the French SOCOM as well as we created a military intern directorate to concentrate all the elements on the same place.

This may be the most important slide of this briefing. Regarding Homeland Security, French SOCOM has very few involvements in this part. Homeland security is Ministry of Interior Affairs in France and most actors are provided by police forces, are provided by Gendarmerie and are provided by special internal service. But we are working in close coordination with them and I will give you two examples. We are providing helicopter support to the Gendarmerie, if needed, to intervene around Paris with our SF helicopters, located in Villa Coublay, near Paris and in case of massive hostage operation, we can be in support of Gendarmerie, if needed. Regarding the missions we can conduct abroad, there are two categories. First of all, the clandestine part and that has to be very clear for everybody here. In France, there is a specific agency working for clandestine missions and it is not the mission of the French SOCOM. It is totally separated. So we are in touch with them because we are sometimes on the same fields but we are not working together, we are not acting together. So we are working abroad and we are working mainly focussed on offensive action. Helped by the intelligence service, as I have mentioned before, the creation of Military Intelligence Directorate, we are working in close coordination with them but the focus of French SOCOM is offensive action abroad.

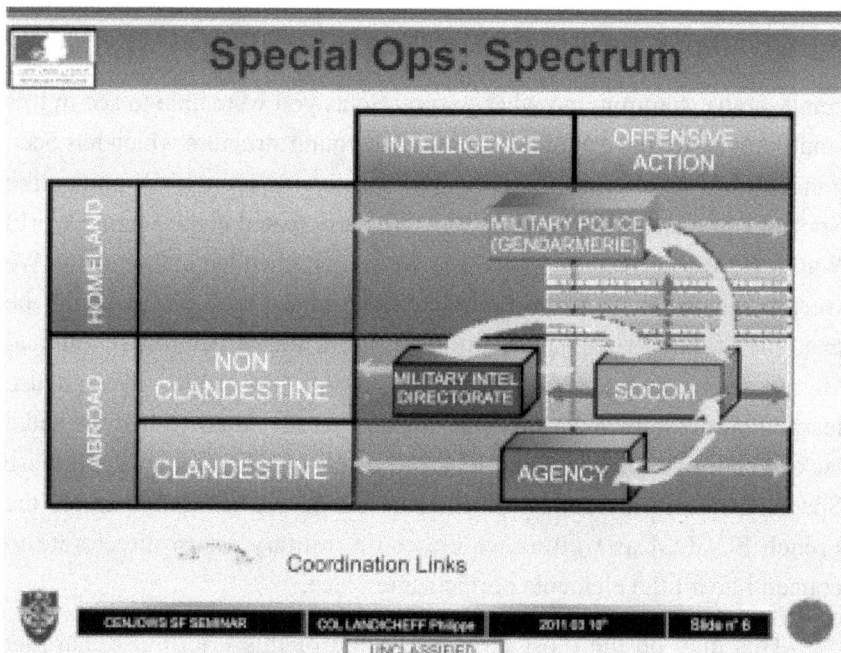

What are our Special Operations' characteristics? As it has been mentioned earlier by other speakers, Special Forces in France are involved for strong political commitment. So we are reaching for strategic objectives. For that we need a short chain of command with political and military control as far as possible but we always keep in mind, the reversibility as far as we can. Regarding approach, most of the operations are confidential before commencement of the operation, during the operation and some of them are also confidential after the operation. So, it is really an interesting point to maintain, to control the information that can be sent by our own soldiers who have internet access on their mobile phones. What we need, in our preferred view, is a lot of autonomy, capability. That is why we built our joint system in order to be able to conduct our own Special Forces, our mission from A to Z and then the last point is of course the training and equipment at as high a level as possible. Why I am saying that is because we are always employed at a very short notice. Sometimes we have to send Special Forces with a notice of 24 hours. That is why we have to be ready, we have to play, and we have to work with a crew and be ready to move in helicopters to a particular site. We have to be equipped with the latest technology innovation. This is the main difference between conventional forces and Special Forces. When we send conventional regiments in Afghanistan, we have to work for six months to be prepared to be sent. So you have to compare this to our notice that sometimes can be 24 hours. So to sum up, our operational characteristic is in operational freedom of action to CHOD.

What are the objectives of this French SOCOM? It is to federate the Special Forces from each service, to promote their use and to adapt and to enhance their capabilities and the mission is very close to the previous mission present here. It is to plan, to coordinate and to conduct actions, performed by Special Forces units in order to reach military and para-military objectives ordered by our Chief of Defence Staff. So ours is a very important part and this is just to highlight that French SOCOM is an operational command and services are provided to Special Forces by the French SOCOM to conduct special operations. It is an original system. Our French SOCOM is a small structure. We are 80 people in Villa Coublay close to Paris in a joint headquarter and the most part of this headquarter is the operational part, dealing with all the plans we can prepare for the future. And I just want to pause on this point. You have may be heard about the operation we conducted in Male on the 8th January, trying to liberate two hostages released in Niger the day before. The two hostages were captured in a restaurant in Niyame at 2200 hours on the 7th of January. The French SOCOM was able to intervene the day after, on the 8th of January 2011, at 7000 kilometers from Paris with two tactical aircrafts, with helicopters, with paratroopers and with people on the ground. And that was possible because we are joint and because this plan was not made during the night; it had been thought of before. This plan was prepared at the end of September, 2010 and was conducted in January, 2011. But I will come back to this subject later on. On this crew, we are 80 people, but I would like to insist on one point, we are working with lot of reservist people. We are 150 people belonging to the soft reserve and there are people at the high level, working in different branches that we cannot have in our home defence. So we have experts in energy, in water, in theoritical approach, in industry in order to provide us a bigger place. But where is the SOCOM positioned? As I mentioned our HQ is in Villa Coublay but our SOCOM Commander, General Beth has two offices. One in our headquarters and the second one very close to our CHOD because he is the personal adviser. So the SOCOM Commander can suggest to him, about how we can use the Special Forces. So he is his personal adviser and of course we are also linked to the global operations channel. As you see on this slide, the manpower is first provided by the three different services. So the responsibility of the organic services is to recruit, to equip, and to train the Special Forces in order to be ready to offer Special Forces, ready to conduct special operation. This is the theory. In fact the French SOCOM is involved more and more in organic responsibility because we need to have global coherence to equip our forces, to train them and specially when the training involves more than one component. So French SOCOM's mission is to plan and conduct special operation and services provider to these Special Forces. French SOCOM is not a fourth service as we can see in some countries. It is a joint component and this joint component comes into being when there is an operation. Before that the Special Forces are under the operational control of their own service. And when they are asked for special operation, they are under op control of the SOCOM Commander.

Regarding the interoperability, first of all because we are joint, we have to be interoperable on our national area. But we are also involved in a European Mission. We participated in EUFOR Congo Mission. We participated in EUFOR Chad Mission; we are involved in Afghanistan with

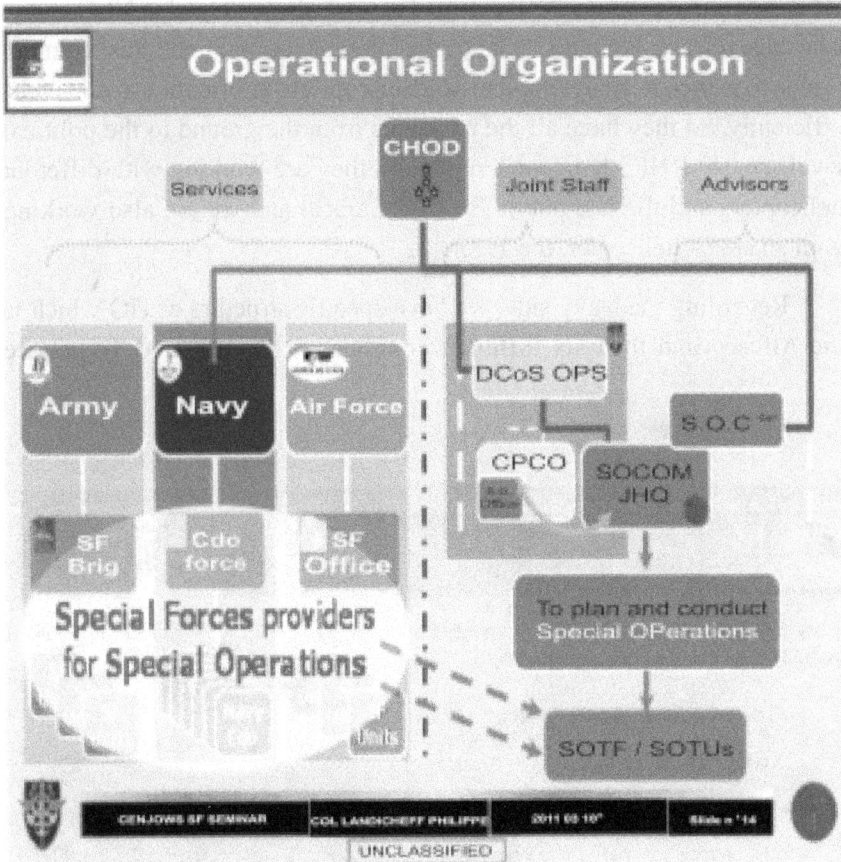

ISAF and OEF. For that we have to be interoperable and sometimes it is said that we have some difficulties to follow. Here on this map, you have the location of different units and I won't spend more time on this slide.

What are the major missions of our units? The three services provide the units. From the Army side, three regiments, one regiment is named 1st RPIMa, which is focussed on action mission. The second regiment is 13me RDP, which is intelligence gathering. The third regiment is the 4th RHFS is the regiment with our Special Forces helicopters.

From the 1st RPIMa you can see on the picture below, the different missions they carry out, they are focussed on direct action so they are able to conduct mounted or dismounted long range infiltration patrol, commando raids and extraction. They are experts in sniping and counter sniping and in urban special actions and VIP escort. They are also involved in NEO and in a hostage release. For the 13me RDP, the intelligence regiment; this regiment is able to gather, to analyse and to send appropriate information at all levels, efficiently. So they have all the packages from the ground to the political level. For 4th RHFS helicopter regiment, they are working with different helicopters and the last one is EC 725 Caracal and we are also working with an attack helicopter, the Tiger.

Regarding the Navy side, we have specific structure as HQ which is the Alfusco and then six different commandos. Jaubert and Trepel are specialised in maritime counter-terrorism. For de Penfentenyo, the main task is intelligence on the naval aspects. For de Montfort, its main task is neutralisation, so they provide all the fire support. And Hubert is our navy sea commando located in south of the France. Kilffer was created two years ago and his mission is to provide an HQ to participate in C-II and also this commando is involved in all the technical initiative we can have. For example, we were involved in IED protection just keeping in mind that our losses in Afghanistan are 50% due to IED blasts, which was a really a big concern for us. And we are working with UAVs and with the dog component. We are working with dogs, who are able to find IEDs, weapons, and ammunition hidden in the area.

For the Air Force unit, there are three units and one commando unit, which is really focussed on the air land integration. One tactical aircraft -

Jaupert- Trepel

Assault and Maritime Counter Terrorism (MCT)

- NEO
- Hostage release ops
- Ship assault
- Combat in closed environment

Squad One and one helicopter- Squad One. We are lucky to have a dedicated tactical aircraft as squad 1 for the Special Forces. We work together in order to be very efficient in the dealing and we are progressing very quickly because we know each other. CPA 10, the commando from the Air Force is located on the same airbase as the platoon. So each day together they can recognize the voice on the radio and it's really important for the security and for the operational jointness.

I go on to the missions we are involved in and all these are in special reconnaissance and military assistance. And I will repeat what was said earlier, the direct action is the end of all the process provided by the mission. And it is very difficult to give a figure today. Is it 20, is it 30? The direct action is the goal but all the work is done before, so for us it is impossible to give a figure. But the goal is always to be able to conduct a direct action.

For the future strategy, first of all we face a paradoxical evolution. At the beginning of the Special Forces, we were involved in offensive action. Close to the insurgency, the French Special Forces worked with a French resistance. And today it is totally different.

We are mainly involved in defensive action, fighting counter-insurgency. So we have to find and adapt to it where SF can intervene. First of all

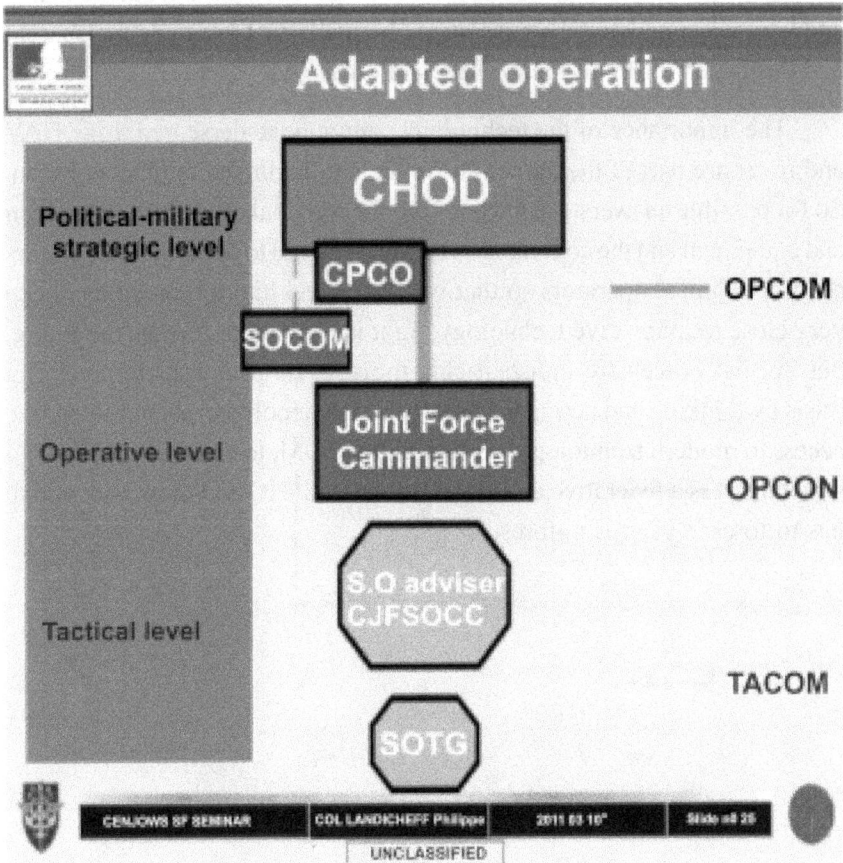

Special Forces are a trend today. We have a kind of SF mania and each country wants its own Special Forces. So, may we have to define exactly, what is a Special Force? Is it a paratrooper or is it something else? And the next point is regarding the state responsibility towards its citizens abroad. We can see that we are more and more involved in hostage rescue operations. We have in Afghanistan, the two journalists. We have hostages in Mali we have hostages in Niger. So this is our political concern, so our SF concern. There is a multiform terrorist threat on our national soil but also abroad, as mentioned. There is a big impact of communication in our own media but also on the media of the other side. And one point which is very important for us is a jurisdiction of actions approach in all the missions that we are conducting. Just to go back to 8th January, the French SOCOM commander was asked to explain to the political and jurisdiction part. What we meant and why we conducted the mission is like that? We have to be transparent and this is very difficult for the Special Forces.

The importance of the technology cannot be underscored. Like UAV and rover are part of the game. So we have to be linked to this evolution. So for possible answers, we have to find the right balance between the man and equipment and the command structure. We need to keep robust operators as also technical operators so that we don't load him too much and keep very close to innovative technology. So it is difficult to foresee the future, but Special Forces are indispensable tools in the responses to emerging crisis by thinking and acting differently, a strong political stance and a free access to modern technology. So French SOCOM, to conclude, is a young structure. It is a federative entity and operational HQ and think tank which has to foresee what is unforeseen.

Employement of Special Forces : Germany

Brigadier General (Retd) Hans Christoff Ammon

It's 24 years ago that I left India as a man who had finished the 42nd Staff Course of at Wellington. So it is really a great honour for me to give a lecture now in this auditorium to my English colleague as well as to my four speakers. I am briefing you now about German Army Special Forces. Well, I am very grateful about what has already been said by Gen Lamb or my Israeli colleague or French colleague. I now cover German Special Forces.

There are some different aspects and I think you may understand that fairly soon. I think the agenda is very much self explanatory. What is the history of the origin of German SF? You may remember in 1994, we had some civil unrest in Uganda and German citizens were captured in the radio station. But there were no German forces available to execute a hostage release operation. Our police force, the Federal Police GSG 9, is definitely designated to execute hostage release operations, but not within a hostile environment. They are police forces not designed for fighting in a hostile environment. So paratroopers then released German citizens there in Uganda. This was the start point to think about establishing Special Forces in the German Armed Forces. And it happened in 1996. But before we carry on, this is again a very specific German issue. By our constitution, police forces are supposed to maintain interior security in Germany. If there is any civil unrest, it has to be done by police forces. Hostage release operations are the police missions, at home as well as abroad. Only in case there is a hostage operation in a hostile environment, the Army Special Forces will be deployed for hostage release operation. Furthermore, you must understand, Armed Forces in Germany are not authorized to be deployed internally in Germany for maintaining the state authority. This is again the police authority. So we are concentrating the Special Forces on deployment abroad Germany not on interior affairs.

What is our concept of employment? First, we are prepared to provide a special operations task group for hostage release operation in a hostile environment outside Germany. Second, we must be prepared to provide one special operation task group permanently on operations somewhere around the world for long-lasting operations. And third, there is always one unit ready on 24x7 status for national safeguard operation somewhere around the world. In addition, we must be able to contribute to combined joint forces' special operations coordination there. It is a really nice abbreviation. But to make it clear, NATO as the so called NATO readiness forces and within this NATO ready forces, nations commit themselves to provide forces as well as headquarters. Germany will provide from the next year on going, for 12 months, combined joint forces special operation coordination centre. So we have to commit staff and other capabilities to such a combined joint force special operation coordination centre in addition to other three missions. But overall this means and this is very important to understand, that we have to provide all capabilities four times within our own structure.

Continuing with our concept of employment, when we are looking for current employment as well as for future strategies and it has been clearly stated as to what will be the spectrum in the future and this already has been explained by Gen Lamb, then we are looking for civil unrest, for terrorists, for counter insurgency, and now the understanding is that as long as we are able to find those who are threatening other societies or our own societies from external areas, till then, it must be our aim to prevent such an insurgency, such an unrest before hand and therefore, in particular, the mission of military assistance is more and more important for Special Forces within their understanding and their role and their capabilities. Military assistance means to support or to train other nation forces. In our case, in particular, Special Forces so that they could support to maintain security in that specific area. And of course, the ultimate ratio, the direct action is the second important element for Special Forces.

If I am looking for a structure, command and control, is in German understanding, always a very complicated system. Therefore, you will see it now, in peace time. Special Forces, as you could see it at the bottom end of the Army Special Forces Command is under control of the Special Operation Division which is directly controlled by the Ministry of Defence and the Chief of Army Staff there. We have also some Naval Special Forces. Of course these Naval Special Forces are under direct control of their Chief of Navy Staff. But they are not under control of the Army Special Operations Division. There could be better solutions. I will come back to that.

On operations, me in the form of commander of the Army Special Forces was the force provider and my successor too is the force provider. He provides, who should be deployed to the joint command special operations which is directly controlled by the staff element within the Armed Forces staff. This staff element is working directly under the Chief of Defence Staff. And the Joint Command Special Operations then controls the special operation task group somewhere around the world on operation. But of course the JCSO has an operational control (OPCON), while the operational commander in theatre, the commander of the joint forces special operations command like we have it in Afghanistan now, he executes and conducts the operation. He holds OPCON. So, to make it clear, the JCSO and a national ASFC is nothing more than a red card holder and administers the operation of the SOTG.

What is the structure within the Army and the Armed Forces? The Special Forces at the Army side are one star command. Next two stars of the commander has operational forces and the support forces and the core of the operational forces are four commando squadrons. Within the squadrons you have experts for land insertion, amphibious insertion, vertical insertion as well as mountainous insertion but they are based on a two years' commando training and therefore, we have our own training wing. So the training for a commando trooper lasts two years. And he is combat ready without further specialisation which has to be added on, than to be executed during his further career. The majority of our commando troopers are already soldiers who have served with other branches. Additionally, we have the wing, the specialised Commando wing where we provide supporting elements to the squadrons on operations who are specialists, for example, technical reconnaissance, tactical UAVs, other technical reconnaissance devices. They also provide joint technical air control teams, as well as combat control teams. They provide EOD specialists and K-9, K-9 stands for specialised trained dogs. And you may remember when I said all capabilities must be available full time, you could see it here. One squadron is the core for one special operation task group. So if you are going for deploying one special operational task group permanently, you must always be able to rotate it with another one and the other two squadrons are then available for national safeguard operation or the hostage release operation. But they are not operating on their own; they will need to be supported. Therefore, we have our support forces with headquarters, headquarters' elements, combat service support elements and these signal elements are providing the line of communication on strategic level between Germany in the area of operation and then forward in the AOR to the special operation task group and their elements somewhere on operation. And of course we have our own medical support elements with us. So we are more or less auto.

Most time is spent to analyse our lessons learnt, not only directly in the area of operation but also in a reach-back method at home, done by specialists and former commando troopers, which are not that well trained now because they are out of age but they could be used as analysts. What is to be changed, what has to be developed further and what has to be done in other aspects, needs to be seen. So concept development and experimentation is done under control of the Commander of the Army Special Forces. And now we are changing to a different aspect.

The structure which you have seen is not capable of maintaining and running an operation like a strike force outside somewhere around the world. So they always need support from other services. Therefore, we have designated direct support within the other services of course. Air transport capacity for long range distances. This is definitely not the UAV but it is the B105, the little bird which we use, we call it the Super or the CH 53 for transport in theatres over longer distances. We have always cooperated very closely with our colleagues from the Navy. We do need fire support if it is necessary by our friends from the conventional forces. We do need specialised infantry; we have difference between Special Forces and specialised infantry, which of course are our paratroopers and we do need additional medical support. But this is, for us, the most important element and it was stressed by my first speaker as well, intelligence.

As it was said by Gen Eizenberg, 80% of special operations are under the surface. Preparation, planning and intelligence gathering and intelligence protection and we cannot express this enough. If you are not able to find those elements which hamper your operations, which fight with you, if you are not able to find who are the guys who are responsible for that, you will miss your mission. And, therefore, intelligence is the most important element and we have to declare and conjugate the intelligence to all levels of commands. It starts with a strategic level. You always need intelligence even if you are working at the squadron level as Special Operation Force, strategic intelligence, you need operational intelligence and this is not only done by technical means. Human intelligence, I think, is one of the most important sources for intelligence at all levels.

The missions that we are executing, I think, are not necessary to be discussed in detail again. For this very young Special Forces troop since 1998 when the first unit became combat ready, we were deployed through the various and different Balkan Operations and then from 2000 onwards up to 2006 we contributed an SOTG to Operation Enduring Freedom in Afghanistan and since 2007, we are now on ISAF of mandate, contributing in the special operation task to ISAF in Afghanistan. And if I am looking at the current Special Forces operations and the missions, it is not by accident that partnering and military assistance as well as the liberty of operations against high or medium volume targets is shown there at the top. This is our main effort, definitely our main effort, what we are concentrating on.

Military assistance, I covered it already, what we are doing is very tactical. Forgive me for that, I think, it is clearly to be understood. We are running through all three levels of training- individual, collective training and partnering with a trained unit in combined and joint operations. So what are the lessons learnt? You may remember that there are different graphics which I had shown about our organisation in Germany. And this is one of our most important lessons. In particular, during our strategic review which we are going through at this time and German Armed Forces will face one of the greatest reorganisations, I think, within the next 2-3 years. So what has to be done? From my perspective as a former Commandant and as already stated to my Chief of Army Staff but also to our Chief Defence Staff and the Minister of Defence, we have to reorganise Special Forces structures in Germany. The already existing Joint Command Special Operations, should be upgraded to two star headquarters, commanding in peace time and also on operations our Special Forces. But not only that, these forces which are designated in direct for direct support, a special operation should be designated through that command as well as an organisational part of the JSCO. Whether that would be decided or not depends very much on the positions of the various issues of the Chiefs of Staff of the services but also on budget reasons. We shouldn't forget employment and deployment of Special Forces is one of the most expensive parts of the military budget.

For improving capabilities, of course, there is always a trend to use newest technologies and we must do that. If we would like to find those who are fighting us, it needs the modern technology and modern training methods. For example, I train my analysts within RJ-II Branch, with a terror police office, that they are able to develop profile for personalities and they are able to track persons in the right manner. This was indeed police function in former days. Now it is also a job for Special Forces and not only for those on operations. How to get a hand on this high and medium value target? You may find signatures at the mobile or phones but do you get his profile, his personality? How do you get a face for that specific person? This is the difficulty and not only that to give you another example for the scope and the challenges which we are facing not as soldiers on its own but also as our entire societies, last week on Friday, we had an attack on a bus with US soldiers at the Frankfurt airport. A single individual attacked the soldiers and killed two of them and wounded three of them very seriously. This man never showed up before as an Islamic terrorist. But he was the one. What was found out later, after the attack had occurred was that this man transferred from a normal individual to a terrorist through internet influences, within three months. This is a challenge which we are facing on the internal as well as external security aspects. And that is, I think, the key issue for future strategies. We are not supposed to develop the many new tactical techniques for the deployment and employment of Special Forces but to understand the environment in which our enemies are fighting and to become one of them and to be in front of them to prevent their attacks.

Discussion

Chairman

Ladies and Gentlemen, the House is open for Questions. You may like to nominate the panelist from whom you want the response otherwise we collectively will try and find an answer for you, and please identify yourself as you speak.

Question: Speaker has very rightly pointed out freedom of action, autonomy and no political interference. How well versed are we in our own sphere?

Answer: All I can say, Mr. Sharma, is that we have a long way to go before we reach the levels of my colleagues sitting here on the dais.

Question: My Question is for the panelists from UK, France, Germany and Israel. The question is, are you likely to offer any collaboration with the Indian authorities on Special Forces' exercises? How about your own model of Special Forces, how do you see that model versus the Indian model? And can you offer any specific series of recommendations to the Indian authorities?

Answer (Gen Lamb): How can we operate with the Indian Special Forces, their exercises and the model? I think, if I can take the last one first. I think it is very important that India decides what India needs in its model and its construct. It has to suit your place and time, it has to suit your political concerns, it has to suit the relationship you have with your inter-agency and it has to suit the very clear threats that you face both externally and potentially internally. And I think in many ways that is an exercise which India needs to get its mind around. I think this is very good example of drawing expertise from other countries to see how we view and have so built ourselves. We can then help in that process as and when required but it really has to be an Indian endeavour. I think the second thing we can do is we can bring a degree of honesty to your debate. It is really important that you do challenge the relationship you have politically, the relationship you have amongst your services, the relationship you have with your other agencies.

We can ask the difficult questions, we could say that why aren't you doing this? It is for you to decide. But I sense that your good manners which are well known and well respected would often deny that honesty of debate. And if there was ever a time for honest debate, it is now, because these threats are very real and it is better to see the problem and seize the opportunity before you have to clean the mess later on and then have a witch hunt as to who was responsible whether sitting in the political authority, whether sitting in the military authority, whether a failure Special Forces or whether there is some sense of inter-agency failure.I think in many ways the international community and Special Forces community are a band of brothers and sisters. And so, therefore, we are very happy.

Col Landicheff: Regarding the cooperation from the French side, we are starting from nothing because we are not cooperating with Indian Special Forces today. But I think today we are building the first stone and we are building this cooperation for the future, as a major actor of the planet.

Brig Gen Eizenberg: I think, sir, the decision of the Special Forces, the Indian Special Forces, will be an Indian decision. And we can only help and we should do it gladly. I will just say what we ask from the Special Forces. When I was in the Command of Shaltag unit which is the Armed force Special Forces I said to my soldiers that I know my brother, I want to know the enemy like I know my brother. I want to know his face, I want to recognize him, to know everything about him, where he sleeps, what he thinks and I think that this is the main issue to decide that you want to know about your enemy. It is a must to know first, to understand and to decide and to act first, this is the challenge, as I said in the beginning, we are glad to help with our Special Forces methods. Thank you.

Gen Lidder: Thank you and I would just like to add that the Indian Special Forces are not limping and, therefore, it is not as if there is big huge quantum leap that we require to take and we don't know how to do it. I would like to highlight, that sometime back there was Special Forces competition in Africa and almost 30 countries took part in that competition and who do you think came first? India. So it's in two words, what really we are capable of doing, the type of personnel we have, it's got to do with the mandate we have and as Gen Lamb pointed out and if you have a mandate which takes you beyond your tactical space, you would very easily arrive into that space.

Question (Gen Kalkat). While part of the observation you have already made, that is regarding the capability of our Special Forces. First let me reinforce that in 1987-88, the British Army requested the founder of their Special Forces, the then Brig. Michael Rose, one of the founders, to visit our forces fighting in Sri Lanka and I happened to be commander. He wanted to study the performance of our Special Forces, we had three battalions at that time, the 1st, 9th and 10th Para Commandos and later on I met him in London, he said that what he had learned then incorporated by learning from the performance of our Special Forces, had got a major role to play in formation of the concept of British Special Forces. So I don't think that we are a quantum behind. I listened with great interest to Gen Graeme's thesis and it was at a highly cerebral level of discourse, (has to be on these issues) and of course got the impression that majority of the Special Forces operations are likely or would likely be directed against non state actors. What kind of role do you see against the state actors? In the same light I am not too sure what the rules of engagement by Special Forces within United Kingdom? Do they under the British Civil Law or there is a special law?

Answer (Gen Lamb): The first question on non state actors. I think I whole heartedly agree. You know, in Britain it is famously said that we stole an empire. So we were very happy to steal everybody else's ideas. And we do that with great deal of alacrity. So the idea of stealing the best idea from the Indian Special Forces, from the Israelis, French or Germans is very easy for a British. It is trying to bring them into reality, but in many ways we draw them from others. My reason was to really bring home the point that the fixation of state, it is only state actors who are problems. That is why I over emphasised the non state play. I think we have a very clear role in supporting conventional operations against a state enterprise. We saw that for instance, in a manner, in 1991; we saw it as we went into Iraq; our concern is very real and then realised of Saddam Hussain bringing his missiles in the light to attack Israel in order to destabilize the coalition and so, therefore, the utility of the Special Forces on that plan was very important.

In the recent invasion of Iraq, the idea was to be able to present Gen Franks with a psychological advantage so that within 48 hours between Kurdistan and Western Iraq, he would probably have control of at least the 3rd if not half of the country. So this was the psychological impact on both the international communities. Again that was just part of this wider role which is not so kinetic and therefore our ability to conduct operations in this cerebral space with using forces, where others not so much feared to tread but cannot tread, is where we would therefore see ourselves continuing to have a role of state on state. I think we have a part to play in support in influence, in looking at the nations, whether it be China, for instance, where one can lead to a dialogue, friendships in order to break down some of the misunderstandings which lead to miscalculations, which would be a fateful error and so I think therefore we could create bridge into areas that others can't in state on state enterprise.

Our rules of engagement are tied very much to British civil law. We don't have any special dispensations. And we operate within those. I often found as I went through my career that the term rules of engagement, it always seemed to be a naval tradition where they wanted the fine details of exactly what you could do whether it was how you could operate a radar, where have you been to and they apply same to the Air Force too. But my view was always that one didn't seek to over clarify your roles of engagement. The right of self defence, the right of interposition was often more than enough to conduct operations very successfully in the conditions we have had certainly in the last decade, in 2001 and in the period before.

Gen Lidder: In a lighter vein, the SAS does steal ideas from others when they don't like their ideas to be stolen. And for that I have proof when we asked for Joint Exercise with the SAS, they plainly told us that we don't exercise with any Army in the world and therefore, we can come and train you but we are not going to share our operational procedures with you.

Question: Sir, my question is to all the speakers, including the Chairperson himself. The SF objectives actually transgress the military objectives and more so, the political objectives. Within the military forum, we all are very much aware of the capability and then what kind of task that can be given to the SF, but finally, employing the SF in a strategic task rests with the politicians. How are they being educated about these Special Forces capabilities in the other countries and what are our own ways of actually telling the politicians what we can do or we cannot do? Why I am raising the question was our employment during the Sierra Leone hostage rescue mission. Sir, there was a lot of ambiguity as to who is going to employ at what time frame. Finally it is that the call will be taken by the politician and not by the military hierarchy. So how is it done in the other countries? Maybe we can learn from that and educate our own polity about it, Sir.

Answer (Gen Eizenberg): It's very simple. Israel is not an Army that is a country, it is a country that's an Army. The Israel Army is under the Israel Government. And the Government decides how to go for the Special Operations. And they decide what is the whole engagement. This is the difference between killer, the theory for permit to kill in a certain situation, in this situation you get permission from the political level. It will give you the license to kill and give you the license to act. Otherwise you are not an Army or you are not Special Forces. What you need in the Special Forces is that they work very accurately in a very gentle way. So this is the relation between political level and the Army level. Another motive, the connection between the Special Forces to the other agency, the political level is the only one that authorises to give the order to this agency, to cooperate on a certain subject because all of them are under the government and the Army or the Special Forces cannot decide by themselves if they want to cooperate with someone from the other agency. So this is the relationship between the politicians and the Army.

Gen Lamb: I just had a very quick one which is my Israeli friend put up very interesting slides when he said from decisive to attention, it's a very important understanding because the recognition by the political authority that you are in a continuous conflict, that the sub-national and trans-national threats are real, whether they are instigated from outside the country or inside the country, they are very real. By that understanding, there is a recognition. The need is therefore to be better at situational understanding. Where situational understanding that is required is good enough, there is better understanding of your capabilities and your weaknesses. Don't try and impress them. That is a fateful error. Because they believe you can do everything and anything in a moment's notice without any further preparation.

You need to impress them of your fragility or how difficult these operations are and how often they can go wrong. You need to move them from being impressed to being well informed. And I think that is absolutely crucial. My final point would be this. There is a well worn phrase which says "fortune favours the brave". Now there is shortage of courage in this row. Years ago, a very nice line was written by the Chief of Staff to Penzamire, Cud Mire, Gen. Mire who you may have questioned for his political inclination but you could not question his combatant authority and his leadership. And it was said of Cud Mire "fortune favoured the competent". You need your Political and your Special Forces to both be competent and practice makes perfect.

Gen Lidder: Well, you know our system as well as I do. Our system responds to both the political as well as the military because they are interfaced. The problem lies in agency selection when there are more than one competing authorities and someone has to decide as to who is going to do it. And it all depends on how well your own bosses actually went and put across the case. I know of a situation where a country asked us for assistance. And the chosen agency was the Armed Forces. They were taking time to put their act together because you cannot push conventional forces in action as quickly as you can SF. And the NSG at that time went and said that we will go there and secure the leadership. And the rest will take care of its/elf. They did go, they were allowed to go and this entire operation was not required to be put into motion. And so it was the political bosses who were approached by the NSG bosses who showed them the possibility and they did it. The same thing could have been done by the Armed Forces, how difficult and complicated is it, to go and secure the leadership's approval? It isn't. But it is just he who went out, put the idea across, got this okay and went. All that the political leadership really wants is the degree of assurance of success. They are pragmatic enough to know that you will not succeed every time. But it all depends on your body language. I mean if you went out and said I can do it, you will be backed 100%. And that is how it goes. It is nothing to do with people discussing as to whether so and so should do it or so and so do it. At that time, many agencies were fishing in that pond and they finally selected that agency which they considered to be the best, in numbers and in skill over the MARCOS, who had the skill but didn't have the numbers. So this has to go on because situation in Mumbai was totally new and various agencies had not actually practiced the situation like that. Next time on, my bet is that you would have a far better response than you had this time and this happened in our first hijacking and subsequently, things have been streamlined. This happens all the time. The feedback loop must go in and it does go in and you find things next time around, to be better and better.

Question: I am Squadron Leader Ravi from the Air Force. My question comes in to state and non state actors. Today there is a dangerous trend; I would use the word dangerous with a lot of caution, with the growing emergence of licensed mercenaries in the form of let's say Black Water, Indus and others. They are growing in strength, they are growing in capability and beyond, which are also trans-boarder. Today, the Chair would see in this, a threat, as in the years to come if such houses emerge and countries let such houses emerge and strive.

Answer (Gen Lamb): The private security companies are part of the architecture. It might take something like Group IV Security. They employ 470 thousand people. In British Army, it is 102 thousand. So they are not going to go away anytime soon. What is important, I sense, is that those who operate properly are monitored properly, their credentials ascertained but the idea that the mercenary forces, as you refer to them are going to go away I think would be to misunderstand the reality. What we need to do is clearly identify those who are acting criminally, independently, arrogantly, irresponsibly and putting whatever they were taught, to ill-use and you could see that with drug barons/cartels who are peddling down in South America, again some of the drug barons and you came across individuals there who have been brought in for a dollar, they were just paid hard cash. And then they were quite competent individuals, so one has to be quite careful. But the vast majority of private security companies need to be just regulated better than they have in the past and I sense that is happening at each and every step. Executive outcome is not something you were to find out readily there, now it is a whole different architecture. But they are not going to go away anytime soon.

Question: Most of the Special Forces operations which have been cited as successful models, have been conducted in countries which have relatively very poor retaliatory or speaking capability or let's say African countries or talking of Palestinians. What happens if the Special Forces have to conduct operation without the permission of the country in which it is being conducted and which has a capability to retaliate? This factor is very important in the sense that at times we are talking of knocking off terrorist bases in a country across our borders and what prevents us from doing that probably is the country can retaliate very badly. Isn't that a very important factor in conducting Special Forces operations?

Answer (Gen Ammon): I will answer that from a German view. Our national understanding is that there is no deployment of forces into other countries without United Nations mandate and with our Parliamentary approval. So these are first two prerequisites which need to be fulfilled before deploying as a soldier in Germany. So if you are going to be deployed into a country which hasn't invited you, which may occur, then there is no doubt that if it is mandated that in the manner as I already said, as a soldier you have to follow the rule of international law, law of war and proportionality for the use of your forces and your deadly arms. That I think is the key issue, as long as you are operating within this context of law, I think there is no problem from my side.

Gen Lamb: I just add one thing which goes back to my point. I have made about failed and failing states. The assumption is that all the nation states control their population, control the land. They have the authorities across. You can look at some of them. Take Somalia for instance, at the moment, it is a lawless piece of state. It is ungoverned; it is just governed by those that we would not recognize; which your ability to operate in those is something the Special Forces will have to be able to do. It is fairly simple when you have sovereign authority. You say yes, well come in or not. But in these gray areas which are always complicated, or other ones that I sense that one cannot duck from the issue, because occasionally you find your nationals or there will be some strategic reason that there is a reason to go there but not dealing with a country that it will talk about its authority but it is unable to exercise it. And so that is an important fact that needs to be rolled into this. Obviously in those conditions you are dealing with high risk, and my assessment is that it is too often forgotten by our authorising authorities that high risk is high risk. They all assume that high risk is somehow the sort of thing that Special Forces just do, high risk and they make it no risk. High risk remains high risk. But these things, somehow I think, you have to have the ability to be able to operate in that space because quite often it is not governed that we would recognise at any form of sovereign authority.

Gen Lidder: What do we think 9/11 was? It happened at the number one country of the world. Best process. And you must understand Special Forces don't have to be mil-mil. They mutate to achieve an objective in a manner that will get them success. All the instruments available to US didn't prevent it from happening. Take the case of Israel; elimination of PLO leadership in Europe. First world countries carried it out successfully. How did they do it? It is there in a book. So it is not true, that you can only operate in third world countries which are not organised enough to react. What you say is true that if we are going to act in a manner, that can be anticipated, whether it is third world or first world, you will not succeed. And that is what the SF is supposed to be doing, that is to make sure that they create a methodology which will get them success. There are no holds barred. And the SF operates in a very different mindset. For them, ends are important, means are not important. For the uniform fraternity, means are definitely important because they are answerable to national law, international law, etc. The SF has a very different paradigm and that reverses the existing paradigm in which the soldiers have been brought up to operate.

Question: I am Nicholas from Safran Group. I am French. My question is two-fold. The first question is to all speakers. Could you elaborate on special cyber operations, which may have been missing from their previews, talks and questions? My second question goes to you, Mr Chairman. Mr Barnwal said that India needs a Special Force National Policy. What do you think could be the role of IDS and what do you think could be the role of CENJOWS in framing of these policies? After I have said that, I am French where the SF is highly joint as an approach which means a close connection in the units and the political leadership. So what do you think, in these frameworks and with this approach, could be the role of CENJOWS and HQ IDS?

Answer: I will answer both the questions for you. Firstly, there is no exclusive space for anyone as far as the SF is concerned. Every space is fair game and fair territory for the SF. And, therefore, you can expect them to operate in the cyber space as well. Next is as far as HQ IDS and CENJOWS are concerned. SF operations are intrinsically combined operations. They are joint operations, inter-agency operations. And, therefore, headquarter which are structured for achieving this end are ideal for achieving this end and therefore, that is the contribution that they will make, both in the headquarters and CENJOWS, as their think tank will put this whole thing together; whichever place there is a gap, they will intellectually fill it before you can reduce to action.

Chairperson 's Concluding Remarks

With this I would like to conclude this session and let you all on to your lunch and all I can say is that the SF as we have seen on this dais has a huge commonality in thinking. Except for small little nuances here and there, the thinking is very uniform. It is true that their task lies in both the domains, the civil and military. In fact, most of their tasks actually fall in peace time and the rest of course is understood. It is not the fourth service. It finds fixes and strikes that are its basic function. It is manned by people of high IQ, high motivation; they are versatile, adaptable, technologically advanced and operate along the entire spectrum of conflict. Both during peace and war, they try and achieve national goals and support main maneuver. They can be represented successfully by the iceberg, who says that you see very little and 80% of more is actually hidden for good reasons because if you demystify, as a conventional mind always would want to, you would end up compromising their methodology and there is good sense in what the SAS does that is, it keeps the mystery going and that is how it is unique in its application.

Lastly, despite what the SAS may tell you, of how they won the last war, I will tell you a secret of why the British won the last war. I met a German soldier on the train once traveling from Jaipur to Agra. He was a private. He wasn't a very senior member of the German Armed Force. I had just finished reading the Russo-German campaign and I knew quite a lot when he said to me, you know more about the war than I do. But all I can say is that I was behind Moscow. I was the sniper and hiding in the trees; we could see tail lights of all the vehicles which were plying in Moscow. He said operations didn't go that well, I got caught and I was sent to a prisoner of war camp in England. He said the commandant of that camp, who was a Major asked me a question, do you know why we won the war? That's because we drink tea and you drink beer.

And now I would like to close the session.

CONCEPT OF EMPLOYMENT OF SPECIAL FORCES IN INDIA & IT'S NEIGHBOURHOOD

THIRD SESSION

Chairperson   Air Marshal LK Malhotra, AVSM,
                                   VSM, DCIDS (Ops), HQ IDS

Speakers

Special Forces: A History   Major Genral (Retd) O P Sabharwal
                                   SM, Former GOC, 6 Mountain
                                   Division, Indian Army

Indian Perspective of War in   Lt Gen (Retd) PC Katoch PVSM,
21st Century   UYSM, AVSM, SC, Former
                                   Director General (Information
                                   Systerms), Indian Army

Employment of Special Forces   Lt Gen (Retd) H S Lidder, PVSM,
to achieve Strategic Objectives   UYSM, YSM, VSM, ADC

Special Forces Employment   Air Commodore Isser, VM
Philosophy of China & Pakistan   Principal Director Operations
                                   (Helicopters), Indian Air Force

Discussion

BIO DATA OF THE PANELISTS

Chairperson

Air Marshal L K Malhotra took over as the Deputy Chief of Integrated Defence (Operations) in December 2010. He was commissioned in fighter stream in 1973 and has flown almost 4000 hours on a variety of fighter aircrafts, with maximum experience on Jaguar air craft. He is a graduate of the National Defence Academy, a qualified flying instructor and instrument rating instructor, examiner.

A graduate of the Defence Service Staff College and has undergone the Higher Command course at College of Combat, Mhow. He has held several important field and staff appointments which include Commanding Officer of a Fighter Squadron, Chief Operations Officer of a Fighter Base in an active Command, Directing Staff at College of Air Warfare, Command of a Tactical unit in Eastern Air Command, and important staff appointments in the Dte of Personnel (Officers) at Air Headquarters. He has commanded the premier Fighter Base, at Ambala, and has held the coveted appointment of Assistant Chief of the Air Staff (Personnel Officers).

Prior to assuming the present appointment of Deputy Chief of Integrated Defence Staff (Operations), he has served as Senior Air Staff Officer, looking after operations in the Eastern theatre. During his tenure as Senior Staff Officer EAC, EAC has witnessed various changes in the operational philosophy.

Speakers

Major Gen (Retd) OP Sabharwal, SM, former GOC, 6 Mountain Division, Indian Army. He was commissioned in the 1/3 Gurkha Rifles of the Indian Army in June 1955 and later volunteered for the Parachute Regiment. He has taken active part in the counter insurgency operations in Northeast India - in Nagaland (1955-57) and the Mizo Hills (1966-68). One of the raids on a guerrilla stronghold in the Mizo Hills earned him the Sena Medal. He saw action in 1962 against China and in 1965 and 1971, against Pakistan. He was Mentioned-in-Despatches for gallantry in battle, as Commanding Officer of 9 Para Commandos.

A graduate of the Defence Services Staff College, Wellington, India, he was the first Indian officer to receive the International Research Fellowship at the Defence University of Washington DC, in 1983. During his tenure as India's Military and Naval Attaché in Washington, DC for over three years, he was made honorary citizen of the State of Tennessee and the city of El Paso, Texas, USA. Major General Sabharwal has also commanded 50 Independent Parachute Brigade and 6 Mountain Division.

Lt Gen (Retd) PC Katoch, PVSM, UYSM, AVSM, SC, former Director General (Information Systems), Indian Army. A third generation Army Officer has a long string of achievements to his name. A winner of PVSM, UYSM, AVSM, SC, CNS Commendation Card, he superannuated as DG of Indian Army in Nov 2009. He is an alumnus of the Defence Services Staff College, Higher Command and National Defence College.

He fought in the 1971 Indo Pak War, commanded a commando company in insurgency area, a Special Forces Unit in Sri Lanka, a Brigade on Siachen Glacier, a Division in Ladakh and a Strike Corps in semi deserts. He served as Defence Attache in Japan, on numerous operational staff appointments from Brigade to HQ IDS and represented India at the Xth International Sky Diving Competition held at Tula (USSR) in 1976.

Wounded in counter terrorist operations as a young Major, he has vast experience of operations in mountains / high altitude and in Counter Insurgency / Counter Terrorism. He is a former Colonel of The Parachute Regiment. Post retirement, he has authored numerous articles on military and security issues for professional magazines and journals.

Lt Gen (Retd) HS Lidder, PVSM, UYSM, YSM, VSM, ADC, former Chief of Integrated Defence Staff to the Chairman Chief of Staff Committee (CISC), Headquarter Integrated Defence Staff. A Commando Dagger he has served in 3 Para, 9 Para Special Forces, 10 Para Special Forces and commanded 9 Para Special Forces with distinction in Operation Pawan.

He has been an Instructor in Commando School, Belgaum and Senior Command Wing, Army War College, Mhow. The General has held a number of important staff appointments to include Brigade Major of a Mountain Brigade, General Staff Officer in Military Operations Directorate at Army Headquarters, Colonel (Combat Power) in Headquarters Army Training Command, Colonel General Staff (Operations) in a Command Headquarters, Deputy Director General of Perspective Planning (Strategy) at Army Headquarters and Chief of Staff in Headquarters Army Training Command. He was the first military liaison officer in Embassy of India at Colombo during Operation Pawan.

He has been Defence Advisor in Embassy of India in Washington for over three years. The General has extensive experience of sub-conventional warfare, having commanded a Brigade along Line of Control in Mendhar District (Jammu & Kashmir), a Rashtriya Rifles Force in Rajouri District (Jammu & Kashmir) and a Corps combating counter insurgency in the North Eastern States of Assam and Arunachal Pradesh. He assumed the appointment of Chief of Integrated Defence Staff to the Chairman Chief of Staff Committee on 03 Mar 2006 and hung his uniform on 01 October 2008.

Air Commodore Rajesh Isser, VM, Principal Director of Operations, Helicopters Indian Air Force. He was commissioned in the helicopter stream of the IAF in Dec 82. He has 7500 hours of flying to his credit, including experience in combat zones in Sri Lanka (IPKF), Siachen Glacier, Kargil and Congo (UNPK).

He commanded a helicopter squadron in the Northeast and another in the pioneering UN mission to Congo in 2003-04. He was a Commander TAC in the Srinagar Valley and has commanded the prestigious Helicopter Flying School of the IAF. As Director Net Assessment at HQ IDS, he has coordinated numerous strategic projects and has authored numerous reports on many critical issues. He is a CAT A flying instructor and a graduate of the DSSC. He is currently posted as Principal Director Operations (Helicopters) at Air HQ.

He has operated with nearly all Special Forces units of the Indian Army in various operations since 1983. He has also trained with the NSG as helicopter crew for special missions.

OPENING REMARKS

Air Marshal LK Malhotra, AVSM, VSM

It think what we are going to be discussing in this particular session is going to be very interesting, especially after what we have heard in the last session on the concept of SF operations in the other countries. Now what we are going to see is what the SF are going to be and what is in our country and in our neighbourhood. At the outset, I will remind you of the rules which remain the same as the earlier session. We will have questions after all the speakers have finished speaking.

All systems have thin story points and weaknesses. It need not necessarily be correct to say that whichever system is good, it has got no weaknesses. No, it could be either way round. It could be a mix of strengths; it could be a mix of weaknesses. And what we would be endeavouring to do is that we should not get into any blame game or passing of the allegations as to why this organisation cannot do this and why another organisation cannot take on this particular task. I think all that we would definitely sort out but this is perhaps not really the forum to carry on with the blame game.

Special Forces : A History

Major Genral (Retd) OP Sabharwal SM

It gives me immense pleasure to be back amongst old colleagues and friends and some of the officers with whom we had fought the 1971 war are also present here. Gentlemen, the existence of the Special Forces is probably as old as the history of warfare itself. In the history of every Army, there have been at least a couple of units, who, because of their fighting skills, loyalty and discipline have been considered the ultimate and above the rest. Special Forces are known all over the world by different names. But they are essentially small fighting forces, specially trained and equipped for a lightning raid against the enemy. They all operate in uniform and are introduced in the battle zone by land, sea or air. They have very focussed tasks and further objectives of the regular forces. They are cost effective and force multipliers.

A peep into the Indian history, for about 400 years shows that we have had some people, specially equipped and trained to carry out special tasks. In April 1663, Shivaji, a king and the Commander in Chief of his Army, personally led a commando raid with 120 men against Mughal Governor Shaista Khan at a place called Lal Mahal in Pune. In 1943, Wingates Long Range Penetration forces called Chindits, went into Burma which operated behind Japanese frontlines that had Third battalion, the Fourth Gorkha Rifles of the Indian Army as part of the force. In 1962, after the war, Special Frontier Force was raised mainly from the Tibetan exiles to operate in Tibet.

In 1965, under Major Megh Singh, a Meghdoot Force was raised and used against Pakistan which blew up a number of bridges, helped capture two pickets, Raja and Chand Tekri Sector and established link up with 68th Brigade, South of Hazi Pir. On 1st July 1966, 9 Parachute (PARA) Commando was raised. It was planned to be theatre and terrain specific for Jammu and Kashmir. In 1967, 10 PARA Commando was raised, designated to operate in the Western desert.

During 1971 war, both the commando units, the 9 and 10 PARA Commandos were extensively used and they gave a good account of themselves during the war. Raid on Mandhol, in which enemy artillery guns were destroyed, was carried out during this period. For their effort, both the 9 and 10 Para Commandos were awarded Battle Honours and Theater Honours beside many gallantry awards. In 1979, when I was commanding 50 Independent Parachute Brigade, 1Para Punjab was then commanded by the great mountaineer Lt Col Avtar Singh Cheema with Sukhi Mann as his 2IC. They were placed under my command to be converted into PARA Commandos. This was to be the Army Headquarter reserve. Their training included deep sea diving and high altitude high opening parachutes. Later on, 21 Marathas, 2 PARA, 3 PARA and 4 PARA have been converted as Special Forces battalions. NSG was raised for anti-hijacking and against terrorism. Today we have Marcos from the Navy and Garuda Commando Force of the Indian Air Force. Special Forces battalions have been used in Sri Lanka, against LTTE, to raid their jungle-safe heavens. Gen Tej Pathak, Gen Hardev Lidder, both commanded the battalion in Sri Lanka. In 1999, Special Forces battalions took part in Kargil. There they conducted a number of raids against Pakistanis, to remove Pakistan SSG Light infantry and militants who had infiltrated and occupied mountain tops on our side of the Line of Control. In June 2000, in Sierra Leone, as part of United Nations Peace Keeping Force, 23 men of 58 GR were surrounded and held captive by Revolutionary United Front. About 120 commandos were air lifted from New Delhi, on a rescue mission which was a complete success.

SPECIAL FORCES IN KARGIL WAR

Employment, Gentlemen, since subsequent speakers are covering employment of conventional war and strategic tasks, I will not touch on those. I will restrict myself to conflict areas and situations short of war. We are already shifting from an era of wars to era of conflicts. Considering India's economic power, strategic concerns are not likely to be restricted to the Indian sub-continent, it may cover the entire northern Indian Ocean and from Africa in the west to Malacca straits in the east and to include Afghanistan, Iran, Central Asian Republic, China, Myanmar and the littoral countries of South East Asia. Our long borders with China, Pakistan and our vast island territories also need to be protected. Special Forces would have a very important role to play in this.

Both India and Pakistan have nuclear weapons which may well prevent the struggle over Kashmir from escalating and because of this, conflict has now developed, into low intensity operations. Jammu and Kashmir is a very good example of how nations may take advantage and keep the operations to low intensity. Pakistan is organising training and supporting infiltrators and terrorists and pushing them to India. It is a state sponsored terrorism.

Special Forces all over the world, including ours, have been tasked to counter terrorism. Hence we must know what is terrorism today. Terrorism is not a random act of violence or a crime, it is not a proxy war, it is war. Terrorism is a new method of warfare, waged through different means, undeclared wars, but war all the same. It is the cheapest option of war, best suited for an economically weaker country. This war has no ethics, no morals, no code of conducts.

India has fought three conventional wars in the years 1962, 1965 and 1971 and our total casualties during these three wars have been 37000. In terrorism, since the year 1983, our casualties have been 66000. Gentlemen, if this is not war, what is war? Every act of terrorism must be considered an act of war and therefore, responded to accordingly. The Principle of Hot Pursuit must be followed. The enemy's soft under belly must be hit, where it is going to hurt him most. In the Indian sub-continent, especially on the western front, this kind of warfare will be the norm and we are likely to have situations more and more where we will have to fight terrorism and the terrorists from across the border.

About other tasks, Special Forces can play a very major role in gathering intelligence, human intelligence as well as signal intelligence. Afghanistan is a very fine example of this. Laser designation of available targets and direction of long range artillery, reconnaissance and surveillance missions deep in enemy territory, establishing foothold prior to intervention, training of friendly regulars, rescue missions, punitive strikes as part of coercive diplomacy, raids on terrorists camps and hide outs are the other tasks that could be undertaken by the SF.

Gentlemen, know-how to produce chemical and biological weapons is available on the net. Soon, nuclear weapons could be in the reach of terrorists and Jihadis. Special units will be tasked to handle them. They should be tasked now as they will be asked to locate, seize, render safe and recover weapons of mass destruction. For this, they would need inputs. And they also need months and months of preparation and rehearsals to carry out this very difficult task. Special Forces could be a force of choice to conducting operations, including across the borders without inviting risk of war. Dealing with asymmetric opponents such as terrorists, insurgents, rebels, Special Forces become the obvious choice.

I think it is time now that we have inter service Special Forces headquarter with Special Forces cells at Command Headquarter level. Col Charlie Beckwith, after failure of his mission in Iran said, and I quote "we went out found bits and pieces, people and equipment, brought them together to perform a highly complex task. Each part performed not as a team, nor did they all have the same motivation". Therefore, the lesson from that is we should give this Special Forces headquarter all the resources, all the helicopters, all the air craft they require directly under their command so that they can perform as one team. At the moment, we have each service that has got a small training establishment to train Special Forces. I think it is time we have a Special Forces school in the country to cater to the requirement of our Special Forces. It will not only be economical, it will also be very good for Special Forces. There is a case to reorganise NSG, the Special Action Groups, which have task for anti hijacking and counter terrorism, need to be placed under command of a professional soldier who has the past experience of being in Special Forces.

Lessons from history suggest that Special Forces who are consulted at the highest level in decision making, produce outstanding results. Our new raisings, I don't think we should be in a great hurry to raise more units. We need to consolidate what we have got. Give them good men, good equipment, the best state of art equipment, good leaders, young leaders. It is man who matters, not men. It is the quality that matters not the quantity. It takes around 2-3 years to train a Special Forces soldier. All SF battalions must have 100% complement of officers as authorised to them. SF units, because of a high attrition rate, should have reserve of men, officers and equipment. Raising Special Forces and training them for the task is a time consuming affair. The real challenge is in organising and tasking them correctly. If they are not organised for the ultimate unconventional tasks, they will undertake the same at a very high cost. On the other hand, if they are not tasked correctly, it will be a waste of valuable assets. Special Forces require a very high state of motivation. All leaders must ensure this. In a Special Forces task, the most crucial aspect of the task is the ruthless, forceful execution. I have seen many well planned tasks failing because the execution was weak and on the other hand weak plans have succeeded because of very forceful execution. Our planning appears to be weak. We plan big but we are weak in implementation. My advice is, have modest goals but be ruthless in executing and achieving those goals. Regional orientation and knowledge of cultural and social customs of people of the area in which you are likely to operate, must be known. Special Forces people should be allowed to visit those areas now so that they can acquaint with them and know them. We should have very close liaison with Special Forces of friendly countries and annual exchange visit must be organised.

In conclusion, I would say nuclear war cannot be won, hence, is not likely to be fought. Conventional war, because of heavy price tag on a new weapon system would be great strain on a nation's economic resources. Just to give you an idea, M-I main battle tank which American Army is using, costs $ 4 million a piece. Mirage 2000 is around 100 million US dollars a piece. B 52 stealth Bomber is around $ 2 billion. And somebody wants to have nuclear air craft carrier, with complements of the air craft around 28-30 billion US dollars. Therefore, it is obvious that conventional war, only the rich or the super rich countries will be able to afford. Combined with this is the fact that affluent nations will no longer be prepared to accept heavy casualties on battle. On the other hand, economically weaker countries would continue using terrorism as a new method of warfare. Countering terrorism will continue to be major concern of most nations. Hence, Special Forces will be continued to be tasked to counter terrorism. We should have special laws and special courts, to speedily deal with terrorists. The way Afzal and Kasab have been handled is a folly.

Special Forces will be the options in situations short of war in politically sensitive missions. In the days ahead Special Forces will be in great demand and many task await them. They must be organised, equipped with state of the art equipment and weapons and be trained to meet the challenges of the 21st century. Mantra of Special Forces could be "daring courage and surprise" as these are the ultimate weapons of a commando.

Indian Perspective of War in 21st Century and Role of Indian SF in Conventional Wars

Lt Gen (Retd) P C Katoch PVSM, UYSM, AVSM, SC

The topic given to me is War in 21st century and role of Special Forces in Indian conventional war. I do not perceive that we will be ever be fighting a conventional war in isolation. Plus, in my perception the role of Special Forces is going to be more and more below the threshold of war and therefore, I have modified my presentation accordingly. Let me firstly briefly touch upon the security environment which is in India's immediate neighbourhood. India borders the Afghanistan-Pakistan region, which is the seat of terror today where you have ideological fuel available and wholly religious fundamental platform for extremism. As far as Pakistan is concerned, you see it is getting more and more radicalised. In fact, the recent assassinations you saw of Governor Tahseer and Minister Bhatti and the aftermath of that proves this amply. If you look at the nexus between the ISI and the Lashkar-e-Toiba (LeT), the LeT is actually the covert arm of the ISI and the LeT has gone and filled up the voids in Al-Qaida. Now that nexus is a great concern to us. You look at the Somali pirates today. The way they are homing on to India; could they be having a connection with the LTTE, the LeT and the Al-Qaida? After all, a number of years back, the Al-Qaida had sent cadres for training to the sea-wing of the LTTE, based on which they have gone on to attack USS Cole. All these actions, we have to look into and monitor them. Wikileaks is reinforcing the duplicity of Pakistan and the covert support it continues to give to the Taliban and to Al-Qaida. The focus of the US, European Union and the NATO and world at large is at Al-Qaida and at the Taliban and not Pakistan per say and that is what encourages Pakistan. The impending thinning out of the US forces in Afghanistan also emboldens Pakistan to continue with its policy of duplicity and it is unwilling to act against any terrorist organisation operations from within Pakistan which are targeting Afghanistan and India. If the Taliban becomes stronger it will be looking further into Afghanistan, it will be looking into CIS countries and it will be looking into India. It is actually Zhou en Lai who, in the 60s, recommended to Ayub Khan, the President of Pakistan, to raise a militia force to fight India and not a conventional war and that is what the Jihadis of today are. In fact their infrastructure started coming up and armed modules started coming up in India early 1990s.

Now what about China? China provides tactical support to Pakistan in its Jihadis' strategy. And that, in fact, has been providing protection to it in the United Nations also for any action to be taken against the Mullahs or terrorists. This is in keeping with China's ambitions, the strategic ambitions which will keep India in check. Chinese strategic footprints today in the Pakistan occupied Kashmir, its arming, training and supporting insurgencies in India, it's claiming of Arunachal Pradesh and the unholy nuclear nexus with Pakistan has got connotations for India. There is a report in the Aviation Week in December, which talked of Chinese Military Advisors with Taliban to advise on how to fight battles with NATO. China and Pakistan's increasing discernable efforts to establish links with Maoist insurgency in India, through the Maoist of Nepal's, through the North East insurgents and through the radicals in Kerela are of grave concern to us. As far as Nepal is concerned, although China spawned the insurgency, the Maoist insurgency there, at the moment in Nepal and Myanmar have taken a turn for the better. But we have to watch out for the future, for example, if the Maoists come into complete power in Nepal, it will have connotations for Maoist insurgency in India. As far as Bangladesh is concerned, it is today clamping down on terror. But there is dormant capability available in that country of terrorist organisations like the JeTI, JMB and the Harkat-ul-Islami, Bangladesh which can turn radical anytime. As far as the Sri Lankans are concerned, LTTE is defeated but it is not dead.

Let us switch to the conflict now. There has been a paradigm shift. As already brought out a number of times, there are clear trends that irregular or asymmetric forces have emerged with greater strategic value over conventional or even nuclear forces. This is the truth. Sub-conventional conflicts characterised by intra-state strife, have gained ascendancy over traditional conflicts which used to be mostly conventional inter-state wars. The trans-national nature of these threats and the increasing involvement of state actors in using sub-conventional conflicts have increased their complexity. Non state actors have added a new dimension to LIC. And they are increasingly acquiring conventional capabilities that were earlier exclusive reserves only of nation states. Technology empowers the terrorists to cause severe damage through cyber, financial and kinetic attacks. Likelihood of them acquiring WMDs is of course a major concern. The spectrum of conflict could, therefore, range from conflict between state, to conflict with non state actors and proxies. Conventional conflict could either be proceeded in conjunction or succeeded, by a period of irregular conflicts which will require low intensity conflict and stabilising operations.

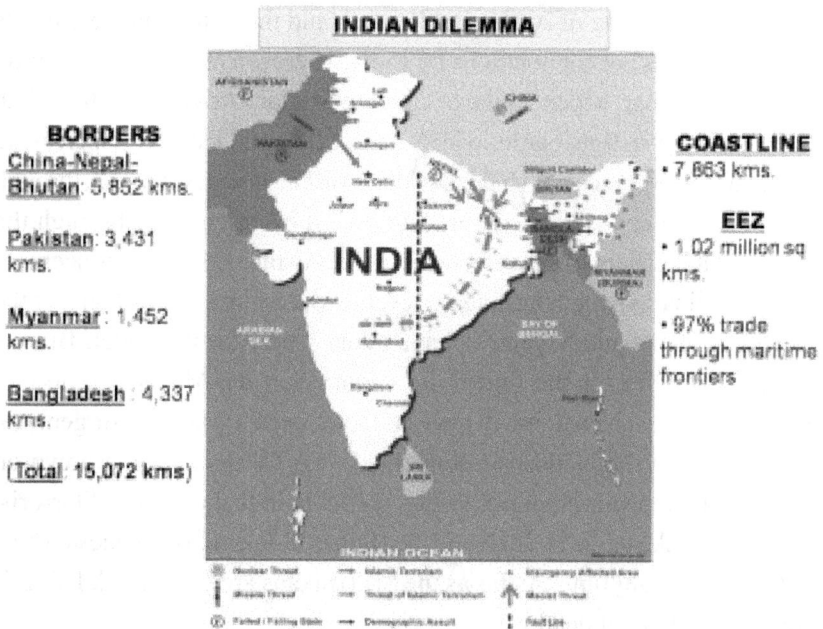

India is faced with multifarious threats and challenges related to terrorism, border management and maritime security, demographic assault from failing states besides conventional and nuclear threats. And India is already in the middle of asymmetric war. We have some 30 odd home grown terrorist organisations operating in the country. And the Maoist insurgency has actually created the biggest fault line in India. There is an urgent need to address these non-traditional challenges. The scope of these scenarios is large with limitless employment possibilities for Special Forces.

So 21st century conflicts scenarios in the Indian context, may be summarised as I mentioned, we are already battling asymmetric threats, windows for conventional war in nuclear backdrop will continue to exist but will be subject to intense international pressure for early termination and conventional war will overlap the ongoing asymmetric war. Both the attack on the Indian parliament and 26/11 Mumbai terror attack, indicate that India is at a disadvantage, relying only on conventional response and politico diplomatic measures. We have not built a deterrent for irregular warfare.

21st CENTURY WAR IN INDIAN CONTEXT

> Already battling asymmetric threats.
> Windows for conventional war in nuclear back drop will continue to exist but will be subject to intense international pressure for early termination.
> conventional war will overlap ongoing asymmetric war.

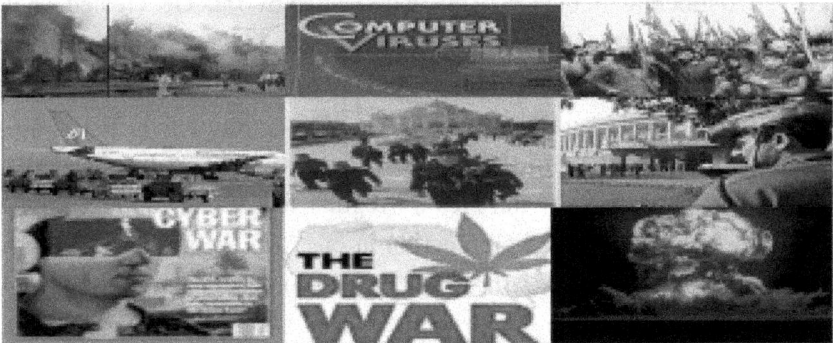

(Both the attack on Indian Parliament and 26/11 Mumbai Terror Attack indicate India at distinct disadvantage relying on mere conventional response and politico-diplomatic measures)

Indian Special Forces were born in 1965, as brought out by Gen Sabharwal. The strength is more than the US forces today but not $1/10^{th}$ the capabilities. There is ambiguity in India on the difference between Special Forces or Special Operation Forces, for example if you look at Wikipedia, that will show no less than 50 Special Forces in India, including all the police forces, Python, Octopus, Jaguar etc to name a few. Now this ambiguity is there also at times of military cross actions. Who exactly are the Special Forces that we want to call Special Forces? They are the Special Forces of the three services. They are special action groups of the National Security Guard and the Special groups of the Special Frontier Force. The SAGs and the SGs of the NSG and the SFF are actually 100% Army on deputation. We have gone in for rapid expansion of Special Forces, ignoring the four globally acknowledged Special Forces truth which are there for you to read. Now this has happened actually quite erratically. At times, the Col. Commandants of the Parachute (PARA) regiment have been able to convince the Service Chief to just expand and convert PARA battalions into Special Forces. In fact in one incident, four Special Forces battalions were created, just in a period of three years which is ridiculous because you dilute the manpower, the training and the combat capability. Post 26/11, the NSG has also expanded many times, although the Army has not been able to contribute much, specifically the officers.

How do the Special Forces of the foreign countries expand? Post 9/11, it is very deliberate. In the US Army, it expanded by 750. UK created a 650 strong SF Support Group. Pakistan added fourth SSG unit only in recent years. With three SOS units, they have been wreaking havoc in Afghanistan, in J&K, Bangladesh and Nepal. Now, when the requirement is more to operate below the threshold of war, it is actually prudent to maintain smaller nucleus of Special Forces and create irregular forces and support around them. We also have a peculiar situation in our Army, which is unlike any other Army, in that in our Army, the Special Forces units and the PARA units are clubbed into the same regiment. That is the parachute regiment. So what happens is at times you will find PARA officers who have not served in the Special Forces, either becoming the Col Commandant or holding positions of authority, where you are actually making recommendations for both the PARA and the Special Forces and also arbitrating on certain issues.

For example, in the current dispensation, there is a proposal that the role of the parachute battalions should be changed to independent small team actions, guerilla warfare, sub conventional operations in conventional scenario and hostage rescue etc. discounting their ground holding role. Now that is an aberration. After all, the requirement of a PARA brigade and parachute battalion is undeniable. Now, who is going to do the role of the PARAs, if the PARAs are going to start doing the role of the SF? I am bringing this up because these are the issues which come up periodically and what happens in the bargain is that the Special Forces concept gets side tracked.

Historically, Indian Special Forces have been used for direct action type of roles in conventional wars, the hierarchal understanding of trans boarder employment of Special Forces in India is short distance, physical or direct type of actions, excluded on a unit, sub-unit basis to assist battlefield victories. There is no concept to use these, utilise these Special Forces other than conventional war abroad, other than just one instance, which Gen Lidder had brought out in the morning, where the then three Special Forces battalion was used as part of the IPKF in Sri Lanka. Other than this, the foreign employment has been under UN missions. And there again India is the only Army which sent complete Special Forces battalions on UN missions and did not employ them for surveillance in the areas of strategic interest. What a shame that New York Times has to tell us that 13000 Chinese are doing 14 projects in POK. SF should actually be central to our asymmetric response which does not necessarily imply operating in units, sub-units or for that matter, physical attack at all.

Physical attack is only the extreme and potentially most dangerous expression of asymmetric war. The key lies in achieving strategic objectives through application of modest resources with the essential psychological component. What is Pakistan up to? I mentioned that there SSG have been operating in J&K, Afghanistan, Iraq, Nepal and Bangladesh. In fact, the first SSG Havaldar was apprehended in Kupwara in 1995. The modus operandi is very clear. You get apprehended, you say I am retired and I have become a Jihadi. The SSG understands that Special Forces do not create resistance movement but advise train and assist resistance movements already in existence. That is the difference.

What about the Chinese Special Forces? Let me give you a brain teaser. It is probably such that some people will laugh. At the first go you look at this slide. What is China up to? It uses the PLA in development of projects including road construction? It is spearheading the massive cyber warfare programme in China. They have established strategic foot prints in Pakistan, POK, Myanmar, Bangladesh and in Sri Lanka they are doing development of ports, development of roads, waterways and the works. In India, Chinese nationals have been caught with fake Indian PAN Cards. Is this the tip of the iceberg? They have established links with the ULFA. There have been media reports earlier that China, the ULFA camps which earlier in Bhutan have moved into Chinese territory, it is for different reason than for political reason that the Government doesn't want to make any such statement. They have been establishing links with the NSCN and the Nepalese Maoists and through them to our Maoists. Now, if China aims to stand up to the NSCN, ULFA and Maoists insurgency while claiming Arunachal Pradesh, can we rule out covert involvement, including by proxy and I repeat by proxy of the intelligence agencies and Special Forces? It is for you to take a call.

Let us just briefly look at the undeclared task of the US Special Forces. Conducted pro-active sustained man hunting and disruption operations globally, built partner capacity in relevant ground air maritime capabilities in scores of countries, held generate persistent ground air and maritime surveillance and strike coverage over under governed areas, employed unconventional warfare against the state sponsored terrorism and transnational terrorists groups globally. And nobody accuses the US of terrorism. Now let us look at the concept of employment of the Army Special Forces which was instituted in 2001. It says Special Forces should be employed to continuously shape the battle field. Now when you say battle field, it does not mean conventional battle field alone. From conventional wars in nuclear backdrop, to asymmetric and fourth generation wars, their employment should be theatre specific as force multipliers to complement tasks performed by conventional forces entailing high risk, high gain mission and having minimum visibility with desired effects. The strategic tasking should be in sync with national security objectives. If you look at the general tasking, every conceivable task that you want to give to the Special Forces can be done under special operations, covert operations or special missions. So what should be the strategic employment of our Special Forces? I would say, continuous surveillance of areas of strategic interest, continuous shaping of the battle field, and when I say battlefield, it implies also the asymmetric battle field because the asymmetric war is not against the military alone, it is against the country and control fault lines of adversaries and potential adversaries. We need to develop both, publicised overt capabilities and deniable covert capabilities in order to create necessary deterrence. For this, both national will and military will are required. Our military Special Forces and the SFF should primarily be looking across the border to nip the routes of the asymmetric threats. It should be a matter of great national concern to us that individuals like Masood Azhar and Hafiz Syed have open meetings in Pakistan with state support, after having done so much of damage in our country, that China is fuelling dissent in our North East and in the Maoists with apparent intentions of preparing grounds for a full fledged fourth generation war in the Indian heartland.

Now where do you go from here? Lack of the integration of the Indian SF has not permitted optimisation of their potent combat capabilities, including and creating a deterrent against irregular war. Our areas of strategic interests need to be kept under surveillance, including through human intelligence to which, the SF can be major contributors. There is a strong requirement of integrated Special Forces command. They can be many models. I just listed out three. The first is that you establish an Integrated Special Operations, Special Forces command under the CDS, Chief of Staff Committee in interim, with the Strategic Special Forces cell, i.e. SSFC in the Prime Minister's office. Model II, establish the ISFC under or parallel to the existing tri service strategic forces command with SSFC in the PMO and office of National Security Advisor. Model III, establish ICFC directly under PMO with SSFC in Headquarter Integrated Defence Staff. Why should there be a cell in the Prime Minister's office? The simple reason is that any trans-border strategic employment will have to have his express sanction. Plus, this cell will be instrumental in evolving a national philosophy or doctrine for employment of Special Forces.

Now the million dollar question you will ask, if this concept is there, why is it not being executed? Many reasons! Firstly, despite 36 years of

Special Forces in India, we don't have a national policy for employment of Special Forces. There is no integrated joint staff structure. There is no institutionalised wherewithal to provide them real time intelligence, there is hardly any joint training and above all, most significantly, we don't have the political will, the national will and the military will. Some of the factors which could help develop the will that we were talking about, appoint a Chief of Defence Staff, which was strongly recommended earlier, effect true integration of headquarter IDS with the Ministry of Defence. Today, it is a separate service headquarters. We should create an institutionalised strategic thinking mechanism with Ministry of Defence which is a void today and National Security Adviser should have military background. Now the void of this has had other fall outs and that is, that 64 years after independence, we don't have a national security strategy; your national security objectives have not been defined. What we are doing is we are barricading our own house. By doing that, it actually amounts to cowardice. And you get the label of a being a soft state. So what are the options today? And since we are talking of cowardice, I would say that if Mahatma Gandhi was alive today, he would have said this, "If one has to choose between cowardice and violence, I will choose violence". So our choices are very limited, either grow pro-active in employment of Special Forces or continue bleeding.

Employment of SF to Achieve Strategic Objectives: Exploiting Opportunities With a Proactive Approach

Lt Gen (Retd) H S Lidder PVSM, UYSM, YSM, VSM, ADC

Well, a lot has been said about the Special Forces since morning. I can therefore condense my presentation very conveniently because I don't think there is much more that can be said on it, and if I condense this presentation, it would just mean one sentence and that sums it all up. It says that "the problem grows when you ask candle makers to invent electricity" and therefore that is exactly what afflicts our endeavour. Now let me go over what I have to put across as a presentation for you.

Whenever mankind has been locked in deadly conflict, contending war machines have realised that there is a need for doing a little more with their conventional forces at their command. This desire on the part of the conservative military mind to utilise unconventional space in order to achieve enhanced effects, gave birth to a large number of war time Special Forces organisations, who exploited the intangible facets in warfare rather than the tangible areas, for achieving success. The British SAS, the American OSS, the LRDG, Lawrence of Arabia, Israeli organisations during their war of independence and in the Indian context of Meghdoot Forces are few of the examples of such impromptu raisings. Most of these organisations as you would have guessed, were disbanded after the war culminated or conventionalised to the extent possible and retained more out of nostalgia and a hope to use them in a future conflict. These forces were never nurtured to the point where they mirrored a challenge to the standard method of waging war. These seeming ingratitude by the conventional war machinery, which benefited from SF achievements, has primary resulted from the discomfort of the conventional mindset to facing challenges towards primacy from an unconventional mindset.

The challenges are severe to say the least. The British Air Force baulked at the citation of British Army, forwarded for the award of a distinguished flying cross to Major David Sterling, since he was responsible for destroying 350 German aircrafts in North Africa. Then there is the example of the British commandos destroying the German heavy water facility in Norway during the Second World War, which has affected the geo-political history of the world. The world would have been a different place had the Germans got the atomic bomb, before the US did. Otto Skorzeny's rescue of Mussolini from the ski resort high up in the Italian Alps where he was imprisoned, is yet another example of strategic effect created by a few brave and determined men, all achieving results beyond the conventional military operating methodology. Similarly, closer home, in a military assistance to Maldives, there was in my opinion, no need to launch a military operation in the first instance. SF and civilians, loaded in daily jumbo flights to Maldives, would have placed the Air fields in our hands and Air transported operations would have followed. PARA brigade operations could have been planned as a back up to force the situation, in case the SF operation failed due to any unforeseen reason. SF invariably presents some more cost effective solution to our politico-military challenges in peace time rather than the trans-border employment of conventional forces.

Low visibility operations are definitely more acceptable to the international community. The SF world has emerged as a no holds barred world, defined by an ends not means, approach in direct contrast to how business is done in the rest of the Armed Forces, where means are just as important as ends. SF operations are necessarily small scale ones, capable of creating large military and psychological impacts. In order to achieve this, SF embodies very high degree of skill profile, where SF personnel usually are proficient in more than one skill. In order to bring to bear unbearable pressure at designated points of application, the organisation has tremendous flexibility in attaching and detaching personnel and weaponry. Surprise, coupled with high technology skill, extreme high IQ and motivation, all combined to produce shock action which is the principal means with which the SF achieves results.

Organisational help, in terms of accurate intelligence and other kinetic assistance from other services and agencies help the SF in producing effects beyond the size of personnel deployed. SF personnel possess, like I said, enhanced awareness of technology, social, political, cultural aspects of target area, they are adapted to understanding media and how perception is managed over communication networks, including social networks. SF persons are pragmatic and do understand that success has many fathers and failure is an orphan. They are aware that the stakes are high and that at the high end is exponential glory and at the low point is deniability of their existence by those who launch them, which would, in some cases imply the nation itself. It is, therefore, true that SF survivability is a result of a complex set of factors which include degree of organisational support, uniqueness of action, non-predictability and surprise. Lastly, a never say die attitude and the will to prevail under all circumstances.

Now coming down to tasking, in my opinion, the desire to pin down SF to pre-ordained task is a dangerous trend since it attempts to demystify the mysterious. This places the force under grave risk and also militates against successful accomplishment of the task. The anxiety of the conventional military mindset, which is comfortable, dealing with the tangible, is understandable. This seeming dichotomy between the employed and the employer can be reduced if the employers define the operating space geographically and functionally and structure and SF based on capability and thereafter leaving the SF to devise means to achieve desired ends. The contours of the operating space for the Indian SF from which the SF tasking in my opinion can be derived, are firstly, likely areas of operations. The area where the SF can be employed in the Indian context are our area of influence first, India's territorial space and 30 km belt beyond our borders on the continental shelf. This is the space in which India has traditionally sought to create operational as well as tactical effects. Then to our EEZ and extending it to include coastal areas of our maritime neighbours, in case inimical activity emanates from the shores against India.

Operating Environment and Impact of Technology. Technology today has shrunk the world. This has increased the span of our area of interest as well as enlarged the areas we can influence. Our SF needs to be provided capability to operate effortlessly in our areas of influence and interest. There is an increased awareness that the military of each country must provide the full operational capability, i.e. across the nuclear, conventional, sub-conventional fields. In this respect, asymmetric situation unfortunately exists in the South Asian sub-continent which needs to be rectified urgently in case India is to create primacy for itself in the South Asian Region. Both China and Pakistan have a fully activated conflict spectrum. So does the US which is the only other country capable of intervening in any region of the world. India, to date has only activated the nuclear and the conventional spectrum, as well as the defensive part of the sub-conventional space. There is an urgent need to, therefore, activate the offensive sub-conventional response, so that India's full potential is brought to bear against inimical forces. Traditionally the SF, along with intelligence agencies, are the principal components which activate the offensive sub-conventional part of the conflict spectrum. Usually, the SF operations in this part are covert in nature and provide deniability in case of adverse international pressures.

Synergised SF Capability. India has a plethora of SF. All of them are operating in different organisations. In order to generate a total SF capability there is a need to structure the SF so that the entire SF spectrum can be synergised by one agency. This would be cost effective. SF tasks would necessarily span from gathering intelligence through the entire spectrum of conflict over the designated operational space.

Emerging Trends in Warfare. The demise of bipolar world and the inability of the sole surviving super power to act as a global policeman has resulted in a world with many conflicts. High lethality, enhanced situational awareness, ability to communicate instantly has enhanced the cost of war in terms of the lethality in men and material thus limiting the use of conventional and nuclear forces. The international community's concern for humanitarian issues is an important consideration. These combined with the issues mentioned earlier has pushed war and armed conflict towards the lower end of the conflict spectrum, i.e. the sub-conventional part. The shift in sub-conventional spectrum has been created by blurring the lines between combatants and non combatants. A divide so assiduously created after the Second World War by the international community through the Geneva conventions. This was done for protecting the civil populations from the horrors of war. Since high lethality precludes the employment of conventional forces and air capability, conflict resolution now calls for precision strikes with minimum collateral damage. Targets in this spectrum are leadership, militant cells, armed caches etc. SF is the only organisation capable of responding successfully to the challenges posed from amongst the population. They, therefore, have emerged as a preferred arm for employment in this type of conflict.

Expanded Area of Conflict. The shift from high intensity warfare to sub-conventional conflict has brought the entire population and its affairs in the zones of conflict. Political, societal, cultural, fault lines have resumed great significance. Exploitations of these fatal lines in these areas will indicate how the conflict will be resolved. Economic and other existential aspects like power, water supplies, sewage, medical supplies, food supplies assumed disproportionate importance. Smugglers, drug peddlers provide the highways in which inimical forces could ride. Fake currencies, "hawala" transactions provide the fuel on which inimical forces live. Smugglers' chains are capable of providing weapons and movement and provide movement to terrorists organisations. The only organisation which is versatile enough to respond to challenges posed in this expanded battle field are the SF, augmented by policing knowledge. Conventional forces are neither structured, nor mentally mobile enough to provide the answers that are required for this type of war.

Matrix Warfare. Technology has made it possible for Govt. agencies to monitor and neutralise inimical forces. These forces, therefore, have mutated from a hierarchal organisation to Matrix control, i.e. held together by higher organisational intent and decentralised planning and execution, like the Al-Qaida. The SF is perhaps the only organ of the Armed Forces which is organisationally designed to operate in a similar fashion. Can the SF due to its mindset, low signature and situational awareness and high lethality, suitably augmented with local intelligence, successfully neutralise matrix cells and turn the tide in the Government's favour? Then there is growth of non-governmental originations like Al-Qaida. You have an objective which is trans-national and you put up an organisation to achieve it. Then there are countries which use NGOs to hunt with the hounds and run with the hares like Pakistan and Iran. It is only a matter of time when countries will be held accountable, in my opinion, by the international community for committing their countries to be used as launch pads.

Globalisation. Globalisation in its way, brings its own problems. Every activity that is now happening on the streets of any country has a trans-national linkage ie the drugs, human trafficking, fake currency, hawala (illegal transfer of money), etc. Therefore, a time has come where you have to look beyond your boarders if you understand the influences that have been generated within the country.

Task in Support of Conventional Operations. Now let me touch upon that and leave with you, the maxim which will help you derive the tasks in this spectrum. The SF is capable of influencing the strategic operation, tactical battle space. Needless to say that their contribution would result from the strategic and operational depths since there are multiple organic agencies available with the Armed Forces which can effectively influence the tactical battle space. Tasking of SF can be derived from an operative principle which is to create friction for the enemy and reduce friction for own force.

Exploiting Opportunities For SF Applications. First of all, there is a clear requirement for a national mandate which authorises the SF to operate in both the areas of influence and interest. Once this is achieved, a capability based SF can be structured to achieve strategic operational and tactical effects.

Organisation. The SF at present is organised to act in support of conventional operations on the continental shelf. For this, the present method of command and control is adequate. In order to extend our reach to encompass Indian areas of interest, these forces will have to be brought under a headquarter which will be responsible to the highest political authority on whose behest it will carry out its mission in situations short of war. The headquarters should be staffed to carry out operational planning over the military as well as political, social and cultural perceptional fault lines. This headquarter will also oversee planning and execution. For the successful execution of SF missions, such a headquarter should, in my opinion, operate under the NSA in peace time, since the NSA has trans-ministerial mandate and can ensure entire governmental and intelligence support. During war, this headquarter should revert back to the CISC for employment.

Doctrinal Support. Once the first two have been sorted out, there is a requirement for putting up a doctrine to support SF operation. This will help in synergising SF action. SF operations are usually inter-agency supported and follow directive style of command.

Training. SF training as they are operating in small sizes is unique and bound by secrecy. Training has to hone independent thinking and the ends oriented type of thinking, without too much emphasis on the process. With this I rest my case. I know that I have left yawning gaps in my presentation. This I would attempt to fill during the Question-Answer session.

Special Forces Employment Philosophy of China and Pakistan

Air Commodore Rajesh Isser, VM

I am going to talk about SF in China and Pakistan, and their employment philosophy. I will cover China first and we will go through "The Military Strategy, a pointer to Asymmetric Warfare"; some of whose issues have been already brought out by the panel and regarding military transformation. It is not only the Special Forces that China is concentrating on, it's almost virtually 50% of the Army that is into very rapid mobilisation akin to special action. Some of the issues which have been brought out i.e. Special Forces, what are their future roles?

The Chinese, with their long historical perspective and comprehensive nuanced approach, have great expertise in strategic issues. The Chinese People's Liberation Army Officer's Handbook bases its definition of strategy on Mao's thoughts; that is, it is a contest in subjective ability between commanders of opposing armies to gain the initiative and superiority by manipulating material conditions. Material conditions include a country's level of science and technology, defence budget, location of forces around the world, geographical setting etc. Subjective ability is the manner in which commanders use creative ideas, initiative and other factors to manipulate objective conditions to their benefit. The focal point for the broader concept of Chinese strategy in the 2001 version of 'The Science of Military Strategy' is the science of strategy (SOS). Stratagem is perhaps the most important SOS characteristic because deception is a practical expression of strategy. Ancient Chinese military strategists formulated that the purpose of power and stratagem was to defend the state by orthodox methods and to use force by unorthodox methods (not unlike asymmetric war). *Stratagem is fundamentally about deception.*

A Chinese *'way of war'* encompasses four distinct characteristics. First, geopolitical criteria rather than operational performance provide the primary basis for evaluating military success. Second, while serious thought and calculation appear to go into determining when and how military power is to be used, Chinese strategists do not demonstrate much reluctance to use force, indeed they are prone to significant, albeit calculated, risk-taking. Third, when employing military power, the emphasis is on Chinese forces seizing and maintaining the operational initiative. Fourth, it is imperative that China leverage modern technology to gain the edge in any conflict.

Military Transformation. The attention of the PLA is now doctrinally fixed on being able to prosecute short campaigns inflicting shock and paralysis (instead of long wars of attrition) to level the technological playing field at the start of hostilities by concentrating PLA's best capabilities against the enemy's most important assets. The "Military Strategic Guidelines for the New Period", initiated after 1993, were about developing strategic and operational capabilities that Armed Forces of China had so far not felt a need to acquire or have not been able to develop, for various reasons. It is a capabilities-based and contingency-based strategy that sets the azimuth for the development of warfighting capabilities as well as professional and other institutional capacities, to provide for the national defence of China that is subject to larger-order national objectives. In 1999, the PLA revised its operational-level doctrine from its previous emphasis on ground force-centric combined arms operations to one emphasising joint operation in the aerospace, maritime, and electromagnetic battle space dimensions. This new operational doctrine was aimed at shifting the PLA:-

> ➤ From a focus on operational planning to prosecute protracted wars on the mainland to short-duration high-intensity joint campaigns off China's littoral;

> ➤ From focussing on an enemy's weakest forces to attacking and destroying the enemy's most vital assets;

> ➤ From the concept of mass to the concept of concentration of firepower; and

> ➤ From static defences to mobile offensives.

Historical Perspective: PLA SOF. Although the PLA did not have dedicated SF until the late 1980s, it was no stranger to the Special Forces warfare. As early as the World War II and the 1940s' Chinese Civil War, carefully selected soldiers from ordinary units were formed into temporary composite units, given specialised training and weapon equipments and tasked with special missions, such as long-range penetration, tactical reconnaissance, raid on vital enemy positions, etc. After the mission was accomplished, these units were normally disbanded and soldiers returned to their original units. Between the 1950s and 1980s, the PLA relied on specially-trained reconnaissance units within its ground forces, for some special missions. Each Military Region (MR) had a regiment-sized reconnaissance group directly organic to the military region headquarters (MRHQ). Army corps and division also had their own subordinated reconnaissance units (battalions or companies). Although these reconnaissance units were not "Special Forces", their missions covered special operations tasking.

Before 1979, the central concept that guided PLA war preparation was Mao Zedong's notion of "early, total, and nuclear war." Such a scenario was based on the premise of a Soviet invasion of China. Faced with a technologically superior opponent, the PLA would compensate for its technological inferiority with its abundance in space, manpower and time. The 2000 U.S. Department of Defence report on Chinese military power brings out that since the 1991 Persian Gulf conflict, the PLA has devoted considerable resources to the development of Special Operations Forces (SF). It identified the further development of these elite units as an integral element of ground force modernisation. The PLA in the 1990s created a number of new SF units, with capabilities similar to U.S. Army Ranger units, as a complement to its existing long-range reconnaissance forces. This emphasis on enhancing SF capabilities was sparked at least in part by Chinese analysis of the role of special operations in conflicts such as the Falkland Islands War and the Gulf War. According to PLA strategists, one of the key lessons of these conflicts was that special warfare has become an indispensable and important combat operation in modern campaigns.

Turning Point. The Sino-Vietnam border conflicts that took place in 1979 and the 1980s were the first wake-up call to the PLA in its lack of dedicated SF. During the conflicts, Vietnamese SF operating in small groups caused the PLA some considerable casualties and losses. Towards the end of the conflict, the PLA quickly learned from its lessons and began to send its own

SF units, mostly composed of personnel from Army reconnaissance units, to operate behind enemy lines for raid, ambushing, kidnapping, reconnaissance and other special operations. Soon after the end of the conflict, the PLA began to create its own dedicated SF. In 1988, the first "special mission, rapid reaction" unit was formed in Guangzhou Military Region. The unit, known as "Special Reconnaissance Group", was given new weapons and equipments which were not available to regular Army units. Its members of unit received specialised training in field surviving, swimming with full gear, parachute jumping, helicopter borne assault, etc. Each of the PLA's seven military regions (MR) has a Special Operations Group, which are about 1,000 to 2,000 men organised into three battalions. Each battalion has its own headquarters and support unit. Their operations are usually in company strength (70 to 100) or smaller teams. The SF units are also believed to be closely associated with the intelligence department of the seven MR HQs. One important move since 2003 in the PLA SF development is that the command of the SF units has been transferred from MR HQs to the headquarters of some group armies (GA). The table below gives out the geographical dispersion of these units.

Military Region	Organic to Group Army	Codename	Note
Beijing MR	38th GA	Divine Sword	Established in the early 1990s
Shenyang MR	39th GA	Tigers of Northeast	
Lanzhou MR		Tigers of the Night	
Jinan MR	54th GA	Eagle	
Nanjing MR		Flying Dragons	Established in late 1992.
Guangzhou MR	42nd GA	Sharp Sword of Southern China	Established in 1988 as the PLA's first dedicated SOF unit, and was later expanded in 2000 to become the first PLA SOF unit capable of air-, sea-, and land-operations
Chengdu MR	13th GA	Falcons of Southwest	Established in 1992. Experimental unit for digitised army and airborne mechanical troops technologies

China's 15th Airborne Corps (PLAAF). This is not a Special Forces unit per se, but a specialised force which is developing a motorised and possibly mechanised brigade with the introduction of self-propelled 107 mm rocket launchers, tracked infantry fighting vehicles, lightweight four-wheeled armoured vehicles and high-speed assault vehicles fitted with 12.7 mm machine guns, anti-tank missiles and 82 mm recoilless cannons. Virtually all of the equipment is manufactured by NORINCO. Pentagon's 2008 report assesses that China could at present muster no more than 5,000 troops and little equipment in a single-lift airborne assault. The lack of transports could be the reason why China has slowed plans to create a new 16th Airborne Corps. However, it is honing its ability to airdrop heavy equipment. For several years, the military has been trying out heavyweight parachutes made by a Chinese airborne equipment factory, which reportedly copied the Ukrainian BPS916 heavyweight parachutes sold to China. The BPS916 can land an 8-ton load from a maximum altitude of 2,500 metres.

Concept of Employment of SF. Chinese strategists believe that if a war against a technologically superior foe breaks out, the enemy is likely to deploy forces rapidly and then launch a massive air campaign. While the enemy is assembling its forces, there exists a window of opportunity for pre-emptive attack. Conducting pre-emptive strikes against the enemy's most critical targets — often referred to as 'winning victory with one strike' — constitutes the most direct means available to Beijing to convince an enemy to desist without having to defeat his military forces, or to make political decisions in line with Chinese objectives. This tactic requires concentrating China's own chief strengths to attack the core of the enemy's defence and achieve piecemeal victories across the operational spectrum against a superior force. To achieve this objective would require a smaller, more mobile and more technologically advanced military force than it had in place. Much of the research and development, as well as acquisition and training programs are centred on gaining the capabilities to accomplish such a force concentration.

By launching swift strikes with elite units and focusing on the enemy's potential vulnerabilities, China can *deal 'symmetrical' blows at the enemy with 'asymmetrical' methods*. Winning the battle piecemeal means destroying selective reconnaissance, electronic and support systems in order to disrupt and reduce the effectiveness of the enemy's coordinated air operations. Combining information warfare — such as computer hacking — with irregular special and guerrilla operations, would allow it to mount destructive attacks within the enemy's own operations systems, while avoiding a major head-on confrontation. *These asymmetric tactics and systems designed to engage a more modern potential adversary could also be used to lay the foundation for the comprehensive defeat of a lesser regional foe.* When combined with overwhelming numbers of conventional low-tech systems, these assets also could give decisive advantages over potential regional opponents. The strategy would be to use sufficient force to bring the adversary to the negotiating table under own terms and to undertake operations with enough alacrity to preclude third-party intervention.

The level of priority accorded to improving SF capabilities grew even further over the years, as reflected by a passage in China's 2006 National Defence White Paper, which identified *improving special operations capabilities as one of the Army's major military modernisation priorities*. The white paper stated, "The Army aims at moving from regional defence to trans-regional mobility and improving its capabilities in air-ground integrated operations, long-distance manoeuvres, rapid assaults and special operations." This increasingly strong interest in special operations capabilities almost certainly derives from Chinese analysis of the role of special operations units in the conflicts in Afghanistan and Iraq. It appears that Chinese analysts have devoted a considerable amount of attention to observing and analyzing the performance of U.S. and coalition special operations forces in both of these conflicts. Indeed, the Academy of Military Science (AMS) and Central Military Commission (CMC) reportedly established special research taskforces to analyze the role of special operations in Operation Enduring Freedom. The table on the next page brings out the evolution of thought on military doctrine and strategy from Mao's era to the present.

Evolution of the PLA's Operational Doctrine and Strategies

Periods	Scale	Length	Posture	Dynamics	Manpower/-Technology	Arms/Services
Pre-1979: People's war	Early, total, nuclear war	Protracted	Defence dominant	Mobile, "lure enemy in deep"	Manpower-intensive, "inferior fighting superior"	Combination of regular, local and militia
Post-1979: people's war under modern conditions	Major, total war	Less protracted	Defence dominant	Positional defence of borders and cities	Less Manpower-intensive	Combined arms (infantry, armour, artillery, engineering, etc.)
Post-1985: local war under modern conditions	Local war	"Quick battle quick resolution"	Offense: "gain initiative by striking first"	Mobile, forward deployment	"Elite forces and sharp arms"	Combined arms
Post-1996: local war under high-tech conditions	War zone campaign	"Quick battle quick resolution"	Offence dominant	Mobile, forward deployment	Mechanised "elite forces and sharp arms," "local and temporary superiority"	Joint services operations (ground, naval, air, missile services)
Post-2002: local war under information conditions	Campaign and battle	"Quick battle quick resolution"	Offence dominant	Mobile, power projection	Mechanised and informationali-s-ed "elite forces and sharp arms"	Integrated joint operations

PLA writings on special operations define SF units as elite combat units capable of conducting operations that may achieve strategic results despite their small numbers. Most notable in this regard is '**The Science of Campaigns**', which defines *campaign special warfare* as a series of combat operations conducted by specially trained and equipped elite forces, employing special tactics. Among the strengths of SF units, according to this volume, are their survivability, self-reliance and flexibility. SF groups range in size from just a handful to a few dozen and serve multi-functional objectives. They usually operate in the enemy's campaign deep areas, where they carry out operations that are integral to the success of a campaign. They are capable of conducting a variety of missions and rapidly changing elements of their missions when necessary to achieve their general objectives. Chinese writers emphasise that the success of special warfare operations depends upon the elements of surprise and covertness. It is most difficult for an enemy to defend against special operations attacks when they are sudden and covert. This means that to complete their missions successfully, SF teams must launch surprise attacks, striking at unexpected times and locations with unexpected combat methods and means. Given these characteristics, special warfare is timed mainly to take advantage of the darkness of night, bad weather and the enemy's negligence.

Rapid Units. The main ground combat force of the PLA consists of 18 Group Armies spread across the seven MRs. Two of these Group Armies, the 39th in the Shenyang MR and the 38th in the Beijing MR, are "Rapid Reaction Units," expected to deploy on notice for combat from garrison without personnel or equipment augmentation. Another three Group Armies—one each in Shenyang, Lanzhou, and Jinan—are being modernised for modern mobile warfare missions. Four to five Group Armies (Nanjing and Guangzhou MRs) are focussed on amphibious operations. These nine or ten armies, along with several special operations "Dadui" (about 1,000 troops each), the Air Force's 15th Airborne Corps, and two Marine brigades in the South Sea Fleet, represent the true ground combat force of the PLA. The 2006 National Defence White Paper stated that "the Army aims at moving from regional defence to trans-regional mobility, and improving its capabilities in air-ground integrated operations, long-distance manoeuvres, rapid assaults, and special operations."

Special operations forces (SF) and capabilities are seen by Beijing as keys to success in targeting pivotal enemy vulnerabilities and maintaining control of the pace of a campaign. SF teams likely will be well-trained to conduct anti-reconnaissance and C2 disruption operations, involving deep-attack raids and sabotage. These teams are trained in para-drop operations, motorised airfoil parachuting and seaborne delivery; and they are equipped with portable communications' jamming equipment. Intermediate milestones were set at 2010, to lay a solid foundation and in 2020, to make major progress towards that final strategic goal. Within this strategy, the PLA seeks to move from regional defence to trans-regional mobility and improving its capabilities in air-ground integrated operations, long-distance manoeuvres, rapid assaults and special operations. PLA SF units are experimenting with small all-terrain vehicles, capable of being carried internally by Mi-17 helicopters, to increase the mobility of infantry forces in difficult terrain (for example, for reconnaissance units in mountains).

Aircraft. China is also making efforts to modernise its transport fleet. China operates about 13 Russian-built Il-76/Candid transports and reportedly has ordered 38 more. It is continuing production of the Y-8 and preparing for the introduction of the Y-9 transport. The Y-8 is a medium-lift turboprop transport based on the Soviet Antonov An-12. This platform has also been adopted for various other missions including maritime patrol, AEW, electronic intelligence, unmanned aerial vehicle (UAV) carrier, and airborne radar test bed. The Y-9 military transport was first shown in public at the 2005 Beijing Aviation Expo. The Y-9 is a medium-size tactical support aircraft that is an upgrade of the Y-8. It is capable of carrying 98 armed soldiers or paratroopers, or 72 seriously wounded patients plus three medics. China is now in the process of developing a heavy airlift aircraft, which may explain why the PLAAF has not moved more aggressively to expand its airlift capacity by purchasing imported transport aircraft.

SF Roles

Direct Action (DA) & Special Reconnaissance (SR). China's SFs appear to be focussed on direct action (DA) and special reconnaissance (SR) missions. DA missions are "short-duration strikes and other small-scale offensive activities conducted primarily by SFs". The SFs practice raids on vital positions, rescuing prisoners and capturing valuable enemy personnel. Targets for these activities are likely to include enemy command posts, airfields, bridges, weapons of mass destruction and key weapons systems, such as air-defence sites. For example, prior to the outbreak of major hostilities between the PRC and Taiwan, PLA SF will infiltrate the Taiwan island using powered parachutes, helicopters, or other methods and launch a pre-emptive strike against key enemy personnel and command & control elements, to paralyse the enemy C3I network and leave the enemy troops leaderless. This strategy is sometimes being referred to as 'Decapitation Operation'. The mission of SR is to gain information of national or theatre-level significance about the enemy, weather and terrain behind enemy lines: e.g., the location of enemy command posts; reserves; weapons of mass destruction; key weapons systems; logistic sites; possible river-crossing sites; avenues of approach; and targeting data, especially for precision weapons systems. They may also have reconnaissance and security force roles in airborne operations, as well as providing terminal guidance for precision-guided munitions. Small teams consisting of 2-4 people will be dispatched to behind enemy lines to collect intelligence concerning the capabilities, intensions, and activities or enemy forces.

Counter-Terrorism (CT). Like all other militaries, PLA SF would be able to adapt to a large spectrum of missions, including CT. PLA SF units are receiving training in offensive counter-terrorism operations to prevent, deter and respond to terrorism. As a result of the growing separatist activities in China's remote regions such as Xinjiang, PLA SF have become increasingly involved in the counter-terrorism role. In October 2002, a PLA SF unit first took part in a joint China-Tajikistan counter-terrorism exercise. A recent report by the Chinese state media also confirmed that counter-terrorism had been added to the basic Special Forces training subjects under the renewed PLA doctrines. Units could be involved in anti-terrorist operations, too, but likely along with specially trained and equipped units from the civilian police force and the People's Armed Police (PAP). In fact, all three, police, PAP and PLA special units share the responsibility for the anti-terrorist mission and evidently cooperate among themselves. China does not appear to have units similar to the U.S. Special Forces, which train insurgents and run guerrilla operations. Nor are they likely to carry out long-range missions far to the rear of enemy lines and on the same kinds of extended missions that U.S. SF teams routinely undertake.

Equipment. China has ensured that it's SF and Rapid units were the first to modernise with latest equipment. This includes QBZ95 automatic weapons, QBU88 sniper rifle, QSZ92 pistol, and PF89 80mm individual rocket launcher. They also have specialised weapons such as Type 64 silenced pistol, Type 85 silenced submachine gun and explosives and crew-served weapons include QYJ88 general machine gun, QLZ87 35mm automatic grenade launcher, W99 82mm automatic mortar, PF98 120mm rocket launcher. They have been spotted using the FHJ84 twin-62mm rocket launcher in exercises. The rocket was designed to launch rocket-propelled incendiary and smoke grenades. Teams are equipped with PDA sized device that can receive both the U.S. GPS and Russian GLONASS signals. This could provide 10 to 50m class accuracy positioning data. China is also developing its own COMPASS satellite positioning system, which could provide military class positioning data in East Asia region in future. UAVs for reconnaissance and surveillance roles which can be launched, handheld or from a small vehicle-mounted launcher form part of the inventory. Units have been investing heavily in the use of Powered Parachute (PPC) for air infiltration and assault. The small size of the PPC means that it is very difficult to be detected by conventional radar and other surveillance equipment. Night-vision goggles (NVGs), low-light TV (LLTV), handheld laser rangefinders, man-pack tactical radio and video-voice-data communication equipment, fast attack vehicles etc. form part of standard equipment.

Force Projection

African Investments. China began in the early 1990s to assign a small number of personnel to United Nations peacekeeping operations in Africa; the numbers increased significantly in 2001 when China sent more than 200 troops to the Democratic Republic of the Congo (DRC). In 2007, a Chinese general for the first time took command of a UN peacekeeping operation— in the Western Sahara. China has more than 1,600 troops, police and observers assigned to six of the seven UN peacekeeping operations in Africa. The largest Chinese units are in Liberia, southern Sudan, Darfur and the

DRC. About 75 percent of all Chinese peacekeepers serve in Africa, where it has heavily invested. There are reports of another 4000 troops in Sudan as oil-workers. This effectively provides a force in being which monitors and can render help when required.

Sea Lanes Some 20 percent of the 1,265 Chinese ships passing through the Gulf of Aden in 2008, came under threat from Somali pirates, who captured a Hong Kong registered tanker. China deployed early in 2009, two destroyers and a supply ship to help combat piracy in the Gulf of Aden. The ships have about 800 crew and seventy special operations troops. This naval experience gives the PLA Navy valuable experience far from its shores and permits China to project power in an area that is important to its trade.

Protecting the Diaspora. Chinese nationals and installations increasingly find themselves in harm's way as their presence grows, especially in or near conflict zones. In recent years, the Chinese have generally been willing to take greater risks than western companies are willing to take as they pursue commercial interests. The most serious incident occurred in 2007 in the Somali-inhabited Ogaden region in South-eastern Ethiopia. A rebel force attacked a Chinese base camp used for gas exploration, resulting in the death of nine Chinese and the brief kidnapping of a number of others. It experienced a similar situation at an oil exploration facility near Darfur region in Sudan. A rebel group briefly overran the operation in 2007 and several months later, attacked a nearby facility operated by the Great Wall Drilling Company. In 2008, a third attack resulted in the kidnapping of nine Chinese employees of the China National Petroleum Corporation. The rebel group killed four of them; four others were rescued and one remains missing. A dissident group in the oil-producing Niger Delta region of Nigeria has warned all foreigners, including Chinese, to stay out of the region. In recent years, more than a dozen Chinese nationals from a variety of Chinese companies have been kidnapped in the region and eventually released. It is generally believed that China paid a ransom for their release. Tuareg rebels in Niger kidnapped and released several days later a Chinese uranium executive in 2007 as a warning to China for disregarding the environment and signing an unacceptable agreement with the Niger government. In the future, small SF contingents based around areas of interest could come into play as China asserts its growing power.

Counter-Terrorism. Because of the trans-national nature of terrorism, China has been working with its partners in the Shanghai Cooperation Organisation (SCO) to fight terrorism in the Central Asian region. The SCO held multilateral joint anti-terrorism exercises in 2003 and another exercise in 2007. China also held bilateral anti-terrorism exercises with Kazakhstan in August 2006, which involved police and special operations forces and with Tajikistan in September 2006. Central Asia is one area where it will not want to see turmoil because it could flow into the already restive Xinjiang. Political disturbances in Central Asia could also harm Chinese economic interests and assets (e.g., in the energy and mineral sectors) in those countries, or they could link with the terrorist threats. Likewise, China's promotion of closer economic integration between its southern provinces and the countries of the Mekong sub-region will increase Beijing's desire for stability in those Southeast Asian neighbours. It is evident that Chinese thoughts on projection of force to protect its interests are fast evolving. SF-based overseas action to deter, mitigate and promote national interests is inevitable and may be taking place already.

In conclusion, I would say that, China has had a long history of asymmetric and special warfare. In Tang Dynasty of ancient China and later feudal Japan, members of various clans or organisations of mercenary Special Forces operators, called Ninjas, were highly trained in the various forms of martial arts and special tactics for unconventional warfare and guerrilla warfare utilising the most technologically advanced weapons (e.g., firearms/explosives, snow shoes, water floatation devices etc.) and tactics (e.g., camouflage, stealth, meteorology, geography, psychological warfare) available at the time. They were usually hired by rival leaders for covert operations and black operations such as espionage, assassination, sabotage, security details and destabilising the political, social, economic and military infrastructure of a rival territory.

However, Mao's concepts, driven by imperatives of the time, put these forces out of focus for decades. The 1962 Indian debacle only emboldened the Chinese to think along similar lines. It was the Sino-Vietnam conflict and the associated 'slap' that managed to shake them out. While the earlier emphasis was on Taiwan-specific scenario capability building, China has keenly observed conflicts in the following decades to learn lessons and change. The successes of SF in Falklands, Iraq, Afghanistan etc. has in part driven the evolution of military modernisation and thinking. It has been acknowledged at the highest levels in China that future competition over resources, energy and water will demand skilled and specialised force projection capabilities.

Pakistan

Coming to Pakistan, a very difficult topic, that's why there are only three slides on this. Pakistan is such an irregular country that irregular warfare comes very naturally to them. So it is extremely difficult to analyse and go into whether there was a lot of thinking behind what they do. Of course, again this is a very personal view and from open sources. The SSG based on the 19 Baluch Regiment was created in 1956, six companies modelled on US Special Operation Forces. In 1965, the scope increased to a battalion plus. During the 1965 war, 120 SSG were dropped behind our fields to take over those three air fields and deny the Indian Air force. For most of them it was a disaster, most of them were caught as POWs. The only one to escape, he rose to senior officer later on, he thought like a special force and hijacked an Indian jeep and drove back to Pakistan. In 1980, the SSG took on the anti-terrorist role as also Siachen operation which continues. In 1999, we will have to agree Kargil infiltration was tactically brilliant. They could do that but what had they thought beyond that? What was Kargil intended to do? And that's where Pakistan does these short-sighted tactical things very well. It is not able to back it with sound strategic thinking.

They have an element in the Pakistan Air Force called the Special Services Wing which was revived in 1999; it was there in 1971, modelled on the US Air Force's First Special Operation Wing unit and the US Army's Rangers, approximate force of 1000-1400 men. They can undertake all those tasks essentially against enemy Air Force related targets, but some sabotage action also. The SSG(N), which was brought out by one of the speakers, who trained the famous 26/11 attackers, this again, although I cannot verify this, comes under Pakistan Special Operations Command, I am really sure about it and I would be glad if somebody can throw some light on that. The concept and objectives etc. is very similar to Navy seals and they have been deployed in a wide variety of missions, including direct action and special reconnaissance operation, unconventional warfare, which was demonstrated on 26/11, foreign internal defence, hostage rescue counter-terrorism and other missions. The roles are predominantly focussed on a littoral and riverine domain but of course they are capable of a whole lot of things including supporting amphibious operations.

Some noteworthy issues. History shows that right from the day Pakistan became independent and the Kashmir issue came up, there has been no hesitation in using Special Forces or irregular methods. Asymmetric actions have had initial tactical success almost every time but never supported by sound strategic thought. There is extensive use in ongoing counter-terrorism effort all over Pak. In every operation, whether it is the Lal Masjid or that famous Police Academy case, it was the SSG and they came out with flying colours. Repercussions aside, they have done well. There have been hijacking case, the PANAM case in 1973 and another one in 90s, where they were successful. So on ground the 20% that you talked of the guns are pretty okay. But I have this comment, again it's a personal comment. And they need to get out of this mindset. So Special Forces, they need to think soundly.

Discussion

Chairperson

Ladies and Gentlemen, on the panel we are all open to questions.

Question: Will the Chinese use Special Forces to deal with internal situations let's say counter-terrorism or for that matter, internal strife within areas such as Tibet or the Xinjiang?

Answer: While on paper they clearly claimed that the tiny PLA counter terrorism effort, whatever exercise they have done with Tajikistan and with other countries including Russia, all scenarios are outside into counter terrorism action. But it goes without saying that knowing the regime and the PLA and the equation that is there, there is no doubt that they will have a problem in Tibet Xinjiang. All the forces, including the PLA 15th Airborne Corps will be used, but the Chinese are wise unlike the Pakistanis. They would have devised something else before they do that openly. Otherwise, the police and the people's armed police are fully geared to take on anti terror and counter terror operations. They are quite modernised. They have the latest equipment. So if you just ask me a personal view, they will use it if the requirement is there. In terms of the will to use, there is no doubt.

Question: I have got a question for Gen Sabharwal, if you don't mind. You had mentioned that principle of hot pursuit must be followed. In our context do you visualise any implications of this statement?

Answer: This is a political decision which I think should have been taken when first time terrorism started. The terrorism started in 1982 and now it's so old that nobody is prepared to check that decision. But all over the world wherever terrorists come in, you pursue them in a hot pursuit. The implications of those will be at the moment that they do it, perhaps they may react because everybody knows about it. We should have done it long before. It is a political decision and then it has to be done. Once the political bosses give you the go ahead, it can be done.

Question: A small observation on the point given by Gen Sabharwal. He said that the NSG operations should be controlled by the Special Forces' men. There is IG Operations and Training. Sir, he is from the Army and we have got 52% component there which is totally operations and training is controlled by the Army itself. And incidentally today there is a Special Forces officer, General there. That is first point. Second point, I have got a submission to go make, in case through HQ IDS it can go to the Army and Military Secretary Branch, the tenure of the Army component, which is 52% there, is three years, as per the contract, whereas, the tenure of the para-military, which is 48% is 5-7 years and incidentally both the Group Commanders are here. Sir you can take their views. They are fighting with their training portion because it takes about a year, 9 months to one year, to put one chap operational and we in the Army, specially officers, we start pulling them out after two years and Jawans after a maximum of 3 years. If this point could be conveyed to the Army Headquarter, MS Branch then we should also consider this point of keeping them at least for 5 years.

Answer (Air Marshal Malhotra): Okay, talking about your second point first, before I hand over the mike to Gen Sabharwal, this is something which is Army specific but yes, I think, we can definitely take up this point and certainly I think the period of training of one person in the Special Forces is much more than what you are really saying. I think it is close to about two years. And if the tenure is three years, yes I think it needs a definite relook. For the first question I will hand over to Gen Sabharwal.

Gen Sabharwal: Gentleman, what I mean is the overall boss of NSG, as I know, is not an Army Officer. The true groups which go and carry out anti-hijacking and anti-terrorist are commanded by a Colonel and they are very well officered, I went and met them both during the Mumbai attack. I spent about a day with them and talked to each and every man there. My personal assessment was, though overall in-charge of this whole organisation, if that is not a professional soldier, he cannot motivate, cannot train cannot look after the groups which are meant for anti-hijacking and countering terrorism.

Question: My name is Bharat Karnad, Central for Policy Research. Gen. Lidder, I think it's a feasible solution that you suggest putting the SF under the Prime Minister and the PMO. With NSA heading it, but again as you talked about in peace time, the control and command reverts to COSC. Now the problem is that if in the modern era, the lines are blurred between peace and war time what do you do about the transition? In other words you have to have a more permanent solution than what you suggest. The transition cannot happen unless you begin defining the thresholds wherein peace times becomes war time and the control goes to the NSA or reverts back to the COSC. Unless you work that out, that's why I think there is complication, you earlier talked about it, unless you have a Special Forces command, I think you are going to end up with this kind of blurred authority with no one being quite sure who is in control.

Answer (Gen Lidder): Sure, you have to have a Special Forces command and that's what I tried to imply when I said that if you are going to remain in the tactical battle space and the operational battle space, our present method of decentralising our force to theatre commanders is adequate. But the whole game starts changing when you get down to your areas of interest which include entire countries and goes beyond the region. That time this is woefully inadequate, is inappropriate and, therefore, we have to restructure ourselves to be able to carry that out. Now since the trend of what is happening in the world is towards the lower end of the spectrum, it is in that spectrum that most of the tasks will germinate. And that is also a political space and, therefore, responses have to be indicated politically for the Special Forces to act. Firstly, extra-territorially and secondly, into those domains where they have not been permitted so far. So if you set up a command which is high enough, the way the other countries have done, then I feel that as far as the SF is concerned, every bid of support can be garnered for them. And why do I speak of the NSA? It is for this reason that if you are going to have politico-military task, in peace time, then it is best that the activity be handled by politicians and the military aspects come from a senior enough command headquarters.

Now in war time and when I talk of war, I am not talking of the sub-conventional war, I am talking of the conventional and the nuclear aspects, now when you migrate into that domain, that is a domain when this command must start responding to conventional forces and nuclear forces. And that is why the entire centre of gravity must shift out from the NSA and go to the

COSC which for want of a CDS, would be sitting in to control operation. That is the thought that I had. Surely there are different models. Gen Prakash has shown us three models. But each one of them points to the fact that you have to have link up with the NSA. We have choices, Cabinet Secretary versus the NSA. I have found the NSA more appropriate with Minister of State. He has a mandate to cut across all domains. He has direct access to the Prime Minister. And that is why I recommended that like the SFC, if you were to get the Special Forces command under him, it may help us. Our limitations are not from the military domain. Our limitations really are from the political domain. If the political domain owns you, you have a good thing going.

Question: Thank you Chair. Haqqani Hussain who was the Pakistani Ambassador to USA, has written a book, I think more than two years back "Mosque and Military". He has clearly given the nexus between Army and the Jihadi groups. Three weeks back, there was one news item or assessment given by the Brooking Institute of USA, if Jihadis take over the nuclear assets, either with the connivance or otherwise by force and get dispersed and hide somewhere, what would be our response when we won't be knowing their location either through satellite and we don't have ground human intelligence?

Answer (Gen Sabharwal): Gentleman, I think, there is the possibility of what you have said. And the US Army is very concerned about it. We have been hearing of this for a very long time. This may happen and it may happen sooner than they expected it to. Even Bill Clinton when he was addressing the United Nations on a meeting on counter terrorism, he said this is not a remote possibility but there is a possibility of this happening. And I think the United States Army very much on the spot on this. They have got their things what they are ought to be and I think they will take action faster than any other Army on that issue.

Answer: The implications of this are, that it is an international issue, international war at a different country and Army is not going to take a decision on its own. This will have to be a political decision. When it is given, then I say you have to plan and it is going to take months and months of rehearsals and planning to do a job like that. But it should be thought of even now. But most of the Army should think of it. And then whoever has to do the job can do it only if you start planning now.

I think I will just add on a little bit on what has been said just now as well as what Mr. Sharma has been talking about. In fact to strengthen the point as to what Gen Lidder had just spoken about and also that which Gen Katoch has touched upon, we need to look at some kind of a structure which is going to be addressing these kinds of issues. And that structure, what the command and control of that structure is going to be, is what needs to be deliberated and arrived at. The moment we have that kind of structure in place, automatically the fear or the apprehension which you have will automatically get diluted if not dissolved. That is one thing and I would like to complement what has been said just now. There are going to be some responses in pockets, in the hands of the government as well as with the military. So I think we can go from here so that if the situation of this nature arises it is not as if we are going to be waiting for somebody who is probably non-existent to give you the word of command to go or not to go but when a package of that nature is in place, the response would be fairly automatic, if not immediate.

Chairman's Concluding Remarks

Chairperson

First of all, I think I would really like to thank the audience for being so attentive and for the kind of questions that you have really come out with and also all the panelists for enriching us with their experiences and with their perceptions of what the Special Forces in the county and in the neighbourhood are and what they ought to be. I would like to add on a couple of things, may be at the cost of repetition.

First of all, I think, in India, the Special Forces operations have been going on for ages. But, yes, they have been under different classifications. We have not been calling them special operations but we have been conducting them for ages and they have been fairly successful. While talking about some of the perceptions from the western concept, which are more interventionist in nature, ours are, I think, a little more tactical in nature as of now. What we need to do has already been very clearly brought out and I think that some kind of study would definitely go into this. We need to be of course more pro-active. We heard the morning session, where I think almost all the speakers have brought out that in their respective countries, they have a command, a Special Forces command as an organisation, for which I think the case has been made out as far as we are concerned, in the Indian context that even we should have a command for the Special Forces which would need some deliberation. We will have to take a call on that. In the Indian context, I would like to add on couple of things. Our Special Forces are good.

At the outset, I think our Special Forces have been doing a tremendous job in whichever capacity. But the degree of success as to what has been set out to be achieved has always been achieved. I am not aware of any case where that kind of a degree of success has not been achieved. Whether we need to expand a canvass, is something which we have all, I would say, responded positively to and we need to take a call on that. I will give you an example. Very recently, I will not take names, we have conducted a massive exercise, wherein it was decided that we will use the Special Forces in a manner of a somewhat airborne assault. There were a lot of deliberations before the exercise and it was more or less unanimously brought out that this kind of operation may not really succeed. But with a little extra planning and effort and more deliberations, it was put into an exercise-into-execution mode and I am very proud to say that it was a very successful operation. It was something that we have been seeing in the movies in our childhood wherein just a handful lot would enter a restricted area and take over complete control of that area in spite of the Station Commander or the Air Officer commanding of that station, being fully aware that this time you were going to be invaded by Special Forces, thus you must exercise caution, and yet it was a total success. So I think my complements to the Special Forces, it was Garud's and some of the Special Forces of the Army which had combined in a joint operation, into making this kind of an operation, a success.

Use of Special Forces against terrorism within the country requires real time intelligence. It has been very aptly brought out in the morning session, the use of various electronic devices both on the ground as well as in the air, we need to have those kinds of resources in place, to provide the real time intelligence, to make that particular operation a success. We require the proper equipping of the Special Forces with the correct amount of technology. We talked about the Chinese capability by you, sir, as well as one or two other panelists have spoken about this. I think this is something which we need to take stock of. The Chinese capability is definitely that which was earlier commenced with an aim of taking on Taiwan, which has now more or less shifted and it is of more significance to us. The Special Forces would require the desired mobility. They would definitely require the joint training. Why I emphasise upon the joint training is not because I am in the IDS, but I think because it is need of the hour. The number of people in the Special Forces is already very meagre and in order to combine the resources of each of the services or from the field away from the services, we would definitely require some kind of degree of commonality which can only come, through joint training.

The command and control structure would need to be defined. The recommendations have already been made and they are fairly well endorsed by the audience as well as by the entire panel and something would definitely move forward, I presume, in that direction. But what has been most important is that even the command and control is in place. It is the synergy of all the resources which are available, without which, once again we may not be that much of a successful nation as far as command and control of these kind of forces is concerned. There is another issue which would have to be borne in mind that even if we were to have a separate command, whether we are going to have all the resources in that command, we would again need a deliberation. In the absence of that, we would definitely need to have full support for use of resources from the other three services. The reason is very straight forward for injecting these and for extracting these forces, we would require some medium or some kind of a media which may not belong to that particular command. And hence, as a developing nation in the absence of all those resources, in that command if it were to be a reality, we would definitely require the support of these services. Political will to use these Special Forces will come with the knowledge which will have to be provided to the politicians as well as be emphasised upon as to what kind of degree of success is likely to be achieved. And hence that kind of interaction exists with the remaining other things which have already been put in place. Obviously, when this kind of advice is being given, we will have to keep in mind what our own capability is.

We are absolutely truthful and forthright in coming up with what is the capability, what can be done, what cannot be done and that needs to be very clearly laid down on the table so that the later decision can be taken, based on the capability which we possess, not on what we wish to possess. We did mention about talking about the nature of war, which is going to be in the 21st century. In fact, a few days ago, we had a seminar on this particular subject and what was basically surmised was that the war in the 21st century at this point of time very unpredictable. And if the war is going to be very unpredictable, then the very primacy of the Special Forces becomes even more significant.

I would like all of you to take home this thought with you as to what we need to improve this and how we can modernise that which is going to come up in tomorrow's session and that which we will have a look at, subsequently, in the morning. I once again take this opportunity to thank the panelists for excellent presentations given and the audience who have been so very good.

MODERNISATION OF SPECIAL FORCES

FOURTH SESSION

Chairperson :   Vice Admiral Sinha, AVSM, NM & Bar, DCIDS
(PP&FD), HQ IDS

Speakers

Enhancement of Mobility and
Firepower

Lt Gen (Retd) TS Pathak, AVSM,
YSM and Bar, Former Genral Officer
Commanding, 1 Corps, Indian Army

Net Centricity and Secure
Interoperable Equipment

Mr Nicolas Miailhe, Deputy Country
Head, Safran Sagem, France

Options for Selection of
Personal weapons and
Specialist Equipment

Brigadier (Retd) Surinder Singh, Vice
President, Special Project Division,
MKU Pvt Ltd

Discussion

BIO DATA OF THE PANELISTS

Chairperson

Vice Admiral Shekhar Sinha, AVSM, NM and Bar, Deputy Chief of Integrated Defence Staff, Headquarters, IDS. He was commissioned on 01 Jun 1974, into Naval Aviation Fighter Stream. He has flown over 2700 hrs on 18 different types, mostly on aircraft carrier Vikrant and Viraat on the Sea Harrier. He has held Command of two Sea Harrier Squadrons and the Air Station at Goa. The Flag Officer has commanded the Coast Guard ship Ranijindan (during Op – Pawan), IN Ships Saryu, Shakti & Missile Destroyer Delhi. He was the Fleet Operations Officer of Western Fleet during Op – Parakram.

In the Flag rank, he has held appointments of Flag Officer Naval Aviation, Flag Officer Commanding Goa Area & Assistant Chief of Naval Staff (Air). He has also held the command of the sword arm of the Navy – the Western Fleet.

Vice Admiral Sinha is an alumnus of the Defence Services Staff College, College of Naval Warfare and National Defence College. The Flag officer is a recipient of Ati Vishisht Seva Medal and two gallantry awards Nau Sena Medal & Bar. On promotion to the rank of Vice Admiral, he served as the Controller Personnel Services at IHQ/MoD(Navy) and Deputy Chief of Integrated Staff (Operations) at HQ IDS. Presently he is the Deputy Chief of Integrated Defence Staff (PP&FD) at HQ IDS, New Delhi.

Speakers

Lt Gen (Retd) TS Pathak, AVSM, YSM and Bar, former General Officer Commanding, 1 Corps, Indian Army. He was commissioned in the 1st Battalion, the Parachute Regiment in June 1966 and later transferred to 9th Battalion Commandos, The Parachute Regiment in July 1969. 9 Para was the first Special Forces Battalion raised by the Indian Army, post 1965.

He has commanded 9 Para Commandos, when the battalion was employed in provision of security cover to the Prime Minister after the assassination of Mrs. Gandhi, in Siachen Glacier and Sri-Lanka. He has been the Brigade Commander of 102 Infantry Brigade (Siachen Brigade), General Officer Commanding,10 Infantry Division in J&K and General officer Commanding, 1Corps. His Staff tenures include Brigade Major of a Mountain Brigade in NEFA, Director Special Operations, Military Operation Directorate and Chief of Staff 2 Corps.

His Instructional appointments include Instructor Class C&B at Indian Military Academy, Commander Higher Command Wing – Army War College and Commandant National Defence College, New Delhi. The General officer was decorated with Ati Vishisht Seva Medal and Yudh Seva Medal for Service during Operations 'PAWAN' 'MEGHDOOT' and 'VIJAY'.

Brig (Retd) Surinder Singh has fought the 1965 war in Khemkaran Sector, 1971 war in Bangladesh, has considerable experience in counter insurgency operations in Sri Lanka, North East, Jammu and Kashmir and in Punjab. He has considerable command, staff and instructional experience. He has commanded an independent artillery brigade, was the Deputy Commander of an infantry brigade in Sri Lanka and has commanded a mountain artillery regiment in Kahsmir Valley. He was Directing Staff at Defence Service Staff College and instructor at the School of Artillery for two tenures. He retired in September 2001, after over 37 years of service in the Army.

Currently he is Vice President of Special Project Division of MKU Pvt Ltd.

Nicolas Miailhe, Deputy Country Head Safran Sagem. He specializes in international relations. He holds a Masters Degree in Defence, Geo Strategy and Industrial dynamics. He has worked for the French Ministry of Defence as an Analyst. He particularly worked on the evolution of warfare in the 21st century, helping to understand the impact of technological explosion, digital revolution, hyper terrorism, proliferation and asymmetrical operations. He wrote a report on nuclear deterrence after 9/11 in partnership with the Foundation for Strategic Research. He joined Safran Group in 2004 and since then has been actively involved in business deployment, defence and security with the three services and MHA paramilitary forces partnerships and industrial cooperation.

OPENING REMARKS
Vice Admiral Shekhar Sinha, AVSM, NM and Bar

Well I believe that you have had a very intense discussion yesterday on the concepts and employment of Special Forces and today we turn to an issue which is as important as concepts, if not more. It will probably be the modernisation strategy which the Special Forces, particularly in the Indian context, require. In fact, I have a little different view. If you see as to what is happening in and around the world, it is no big war but there are theatres where the Special Forces are more active than the more conventional and visible forces and I believe that a time is not very far when there will be requirement of seamless integrity amongst the Special Forces of various countries in one area of operation, if we have to maintain or if we have to take a collective responsibility of peace and stability. I mean these are the words which are very frequently used and, therefore, I will like to use these words. And in the world of multi polarity, it is not possible for one single country to take on these tasks. And if you see what is happening and what has happened in last month or so, there seems to be a simmering turmoil in more than one theatre. And I don't see this settling down very quickly. And therefore, today's seminar, I think, is very well timed and I believe that there is a reason for us that seamless integration of the Special Forces, not only within the country but amongst the countries, who will be responsible for bringing peace and stability in a region, is going to increase. Therefore, we need to look at this entire thing in that light.

It is well known that the Special Forces operate without the support from either the artillery or any Air Force; as far as the fire part is concerned, the basic level personal weapon should be very light, it should be water resistant. I, being a marine man, keep making a point in every forum, that it must have a small barrel and must be very reliable, accurate, but should also be able to deliver maximum punch. Apart from weapons, there is a wide variety of equipments which could be considered. Emerging technologies enables the Special Forces operatives to become very self-contained, fully networked and enhance their lethality, while ensuring their own survival. So as I look at it, I know there are very experienced Special Forces practitioners here, but I think the first thing is the survival of the Special Forces while it maintains its stealth. Second issue is, having a very high degree of lethality and thirdly, in today's scenario, as was mentioned in the introduction, that we need to be networked with various agencies so that the targeting is that much easier. And I am sure we are going to hear more of it when the speakers come.

As far as the employment of Special Forces is concerned, I was fortunate to be participating in the Operation Pawan, which took place in Sri Lanka and that was the first time that the very nascent Indian Naval Marine Commandos were blooded into action. It is a famous study, of course Gen Kalkat is sitting here, I need not labour on this but it will be good to recall the scuttling of the large number of boats in the Jaffna Lagoon by the IMSF, that ultimately led to saving many lives in that area which we were not aware of at one point of time as to where the fire was coming from and we had a whole night operation where the IMSF was launched into action. They went under water for a long distance, did whatever they were supposed to do and happily came back all alive. As far as the Mumbai attack is concerned, it was for everybody to see, it was on the TV, very well televised. The media really brought it out and therefore, it has highlighted the importance or may be the lack of it, in at least our scenario.

As to whether we do have the right equipment, the right processes, a lot has happened after that, which I am sure the agencies who were involved there are addressing. So the state of the art weapons and equipment are very important attributes of an effective SF team and equipment to be allocated could be governed by the nature of mission and of course the technology which is available. Notwithstanding that, the SF teams always prefer to travel light, because everyone is on their own. I am told that as many as 40 specialized items have been identified for a typical SF soldier. Correct me if I am wrong. I only pick it up from what comes out in the magazines. High-tech systems and weapons have the potential to provide tactical surprise and the leverage, which could prove to be very critical for success of a mission. Raising and equipping Special Forces is expensive, it requires fair amount of funds because you are looking at a system which can get outdated in a month's time, possibly. It is important, that we should ensure that we get the bang for the buck and I am sure that we all have a very huge wish list, but being part of Perspective Planning, when it comes to IDS Headquarter, all I will say is that we should look at the budget and see what best we can buy. We are not a country which has huge amounts of spare money to spend, but I am sure that the requirements are very well understood by people who take these decisions. We have representation from industry and I am sure that the speakers will put forward this point, as to what is on offer and what is likely to happen in next 5-10 years.

Enhancement of Mobility and Firepower
Lt Gen (Retd) TS Pathak, AVSM, YSM and Bar

Talking about modernisation of Special Forces, the way I look at it, what exactly is modernisation? As per my understanding, it is a co-evolution of concepts, organisations and technology. You can't do one without the other. It is not technology alone. Changes in any one of these should trigger a response in the other. It happens even in the corporate world; businesses once they acquire technology, they find, they have to restructure the organisation to make optimum use of it. What comes out as the end product is entirely different from the original. Same thing applies to Special Forces. Take whatever you like, it's not just technology, if you are going to get new systems, it must trigger a change in your organisation. A new evolution of a concept should trigger a change in the organisation and allow you to get higher end technology. Now these are correlated and unless we can understand this, we are not talking about any modernisation.

Allow me in this, yesterday we spoke about Special Forces and others and likely challenges. I would want to recount a small African fable. Every morning, the gazelle gets up and realises that he has got to run fast; faster than the fastest lion, if he is going to survive. At the same time, the lion also gets up in the morning and he says I must also run fast, faster than the slowest gazelle if I don't want to die of hunger. Now you've got to decide who is the gazelle and who, the lion? If the adversary is in any of these roles, you are going to decide whether you are the lion or the gazelle and accordingly what the terrorist is and whether the Special Forces or the security forces are the lions or vice-a-versa. This is something on which you are going to take your own call. One thing we've got to remember with globalisation and technology available and the internet, there is a very common playing field. The non state actor as also the state actors have got technology, whatever they want. For the non state actor, although irregular, the investment is the least, he selects a target with the tools that are available, he invests in one odd weapon, selects a small nucleus of 3 - 4 people and launches it. On the other hand, Special Forces and the Security Forces have got to look at so many targets, so much to respond to and a big budget. He has got to be equipped with a whole range of capabilities, to defeat that one action of the non state actor and he has got to equip a large number of people. So the budget is a factor that cannot be wished away when you are looking at modernisation.

Another issue I would like to put my mind on, actually the Special Forces and special operations are a rather emphasised thing, in especially as far as the Indian context is concerned. It is rather difficult to define. A lot has been said about Special Forces yesterday. Let me look at to my way of thinking. What is a special operation? I would say it is a high risk venture. There is no doubt about it. Its success depends on intelligence input of a very high order. I don't think there is any dispute about it. Yes, it involves very discreet manpower and fire power; this is something that we've got to bear in mind, discreet use of men and fire power, success and failure, yesterday Gen Lamb said, yes you've got to condition your employer about failure. I would look at the same aspects in the conventional field also. If a special operation succeeds, the main plan goes through without a hit, like a hot knife through butter. But should it fail, the main plan should still succeed on its own merit. So, the Special Forces or the special operation is like a force multiplier. On the unconventional side, if we talk about Operation Eagle Claw, was it a failure. Yes, in certain respects, it was a failure. But, it is also said that the inputs reaped especially in relation to the radar and the other frequencies of the Soviet Union were tremendous intelligence inputs that they received during the operation as part of Eagle Claw because the Americans were also worried about the Soviets. Now, maybe Special Forces or special operations are not failures in the conventional terms and lastly a special operation does not bank on reserves. You cannot retrieve a situation or like in conventional conflict, use reserves. So this is the way I look at a special operation.

Now, keeping this in mind, yesterday we spoke about full spectrum dominance. Now if you take the violence scale from 0-10, stone pelting, that the Indian sub-continent has seen in Kashmir would be at zero and use of weapons of mass destruction, or as Gen Lamb said, weapons of mass disorder, would be at the upper hand. Special operations have got to be launched in this from a scale of 0-10. Coming closer through the subject that I have got to address, we can look at modernisation in the fire power and mobility dimension. Fire power and mobility are two basic principles of all warfare. Do you trade one against the other? I have no desire to go into specifics of any weapons system, but the way I look at it, I will address this issue at three levels. The individual, crew served entity and others. The way I look at it, for an individual you are going to have a multi function combat weapon, which is capable, to my way of thinking, of firing a kinetic energy as also a high explosive round fragmentation capability. His weapon should integrate area weapon suppression capability and it should be modular in design. I would also prefer, if possible, that it should have range estimation and designation facility as also a ballistic computer for ruling over errors. The question is, is it possible? Maybe a modular design may allow the functions, may be it may not. You may have everything coming, but to build in sensors and ballistic computer capability may just not be possible. Maybe not now, maybe couple of years later, I would look at an individual capability as also the ability to bring down maximum ordinance on the targets.

Coming down to our context, where we have a number of Special Forces, my recommendations would be, at least they should be inter operable with each other and have one for the individual, a one weapon philosophy. It will cut down on logistics because logistics, at a later stage, will play a very important part in sustenance. Looking at the crew served weapons systems again, I think, they should be light weight, again have a personal suppression capability at a range of about 2000 metres and a destructive capability against material targets and light armoured vehicles, to a range of 2000 metres. One single weapon gives you this capability and it should be adaptable to a regular operation as well as have the ability to be mounted on helicopters. This would be the weapon system I would prefer and not what, in a lighter way, Gen Lidder was talking about, a sniper rifle with a bayonet.

Again logistics is a very important issue. Now, going beyond these individual and sub-unit weapons, let us look at the others, that is the long range rocket artillery, air and also naval gun fires and missiles. The ability to integrate them by way of designation of a target by Special Forces during a special operation, should exist. It would be ideal to have one designator performing these functions instead of looking at variety of designators. Because, you've got to realise, everything that the troops are going to carry is going to add on to their weight. As it is, we are expecting him to carry a far greater amount of equipment, so whatever is done, our common platform makes life that much more simpler. And this should be available with integration capability of using other weapons or indirectly should be available to all Special Forces, whether they be in the Navy, Air Force, or Army, as they exist in our context today.

I would also like to mention something about non-lethal weapons systems. We don't look at them but let us also not wish them away, especially in our context because if you all look at Mumbai when it happened, or any blast that takes place, you see the amount of crowds that gather around there. Are there pro or hostile elements in it? It is a nightmare for our operation. The same thing applies to the western experience in the Asiatic war. The population density is far higher overall than what is in Europe and otherwise. Therefore, you look at certain non-lethal weapon systems for crowd control incapacitation to deny access and clear facilities and structures should also be considered. Similarly, in non-lethal weapon system we should look at certain counter material for area denial and neutralise equipment. Technologies are available in form of kinetic energy, electro-magnetic, acoustics, chemicals others like laser. Because, think about it, what happened in Kashmir during the stone pelting, every time you used ammunition you are shooting a few and creating a chaos. Would a non lethal weapon system by the Police Special Forces, have served the purpose or not? I leave it to you to take your call.

Lastly, now we come to the mobility. Now again mobility allocated, there are two aspects to it. First is the mental mobility which is the function of quality and training, with emphasis on education. Now I think the next session discusses the human resource development issue but I would like to say that the Indian Army Special Forces have taken a very conscious decision to my way of reckoning to trade off quality for quantity. Now whatever may be the reason or rationale, they would know it best but trading off quality for quantity is not the answer in modernisation of Special Forces. The aspect of mental mobility is training. Now while training, the way I look at it, battle drills are reactions to a set situation and there is something known as an Ashland phenomenon, that we have created structures and organisations for a situation. The situation has changed and the reaction and structures are the same. Training is fine initially but as far as the Special Forces are concerned, it is not just training; it has got to be education, his ability to take stock of the environment and to react. No battle drill can teach him, battle drill is just an initial foundation. This is where it completes the loop, it comes in with quality of manpower. If you have low grade manpower, how do you spend time to educate him? This is a very important issue. When we talk about mobility, about all the other means, we tend to forget this. This is one aspect. I am sure it will get addressed later.

Physical mobility can be looked at in the tactical or strategic dimensions, land, air, sea. It is fine. All those things are there and yesterday, during the discussion it did get mentioned that ideally, if the assets, especially air delivery assets are grouped and are part of the Special Forces organisational structure. However if that is not possible, then you are going to have a very high degree assurance on availability of these assets when required. It helps tide over a problem but then what happens is you tend to take that for granted and don't create dedicated assets. It is not a question of a platform, it is not a question of a vehicle. It is question of the value addition which is required to make it functional or versatile for special operations and used by Special Forces. Assurance, high assurance, levels on availability works to an extent, but it is not the answer because both have got to understand each other. They have got to know the nuances of each other, and unless they talk a common language, bringing in people at the last moment and don't integrate them properly, you are going to have problems like what happened in Operation Eagle Claw.

A few other issues that I would look at it, especially in our context, is that any means of mobility used by the Special Forces in our context, specially the Asian context, must have the ability of survival, post operation and self destruct because there may be times when you would not be able to extract them out. Majority should be air deliverable and the training of Special Forces should be handling familiarity with all means of transport that are available in the region on a scale of zero to midway at least as far as land mobility is concerned.

Net Centricity and Secure Interoperable, Equipment for Special Forces

Mr Nicolas Miailhe

I am French and I represent a French group which is called Safran. I work for a company which is called Sagem and I am going to talk about technology. I will focus on network-centric solutions for Special Forces modernisation. Like it was mentioned this morning, digital revolution and technological explosion is infusing massively in all the aspects of our life, including Armed Forces. Generally Special Forces and Commandoes have been spearheading the technological absorption throughout history. Why? Because they have higher skill, because they get massive training, regular training and exercising. So they have been spearheading, therefore, to absorb technology into their way of operating and down the line into doctrine and into organisations. In this age of technological explosion, wherein the digital revolution has brought a lot of capabilities through network, to increase the individual and collective intelligence, there are ways and there are means to provide Special Forces with the increased capability. So I will focus a bit on the French example. I am glad that we have here a representative of the French Special Forces. We were selected, way back in 2003 by the French Government to spearhead the French Army, including French Army Special Forces effort to conduct an integrated network centric soldiers' modernisation programme. After more than eight years now of research, developments, pre-production, small scale trials, large scale trials, adjustment in post trial upgrade of the system, we are now allowed to bring in mass production. So we have benefit of more than eight years of expertise in bringing these technologies down to the last mile, if I can say so, down to the soldier basically. And this has given us a bit of confidence and a bit of expertise in this field.

So what I will do is, I will put some slides across. I will also show you a movie with a scenario dedicated to urban warfare and assault in a village. So when you look at the soldier, some of you may believe that it looks like

FELIN : French Soldier

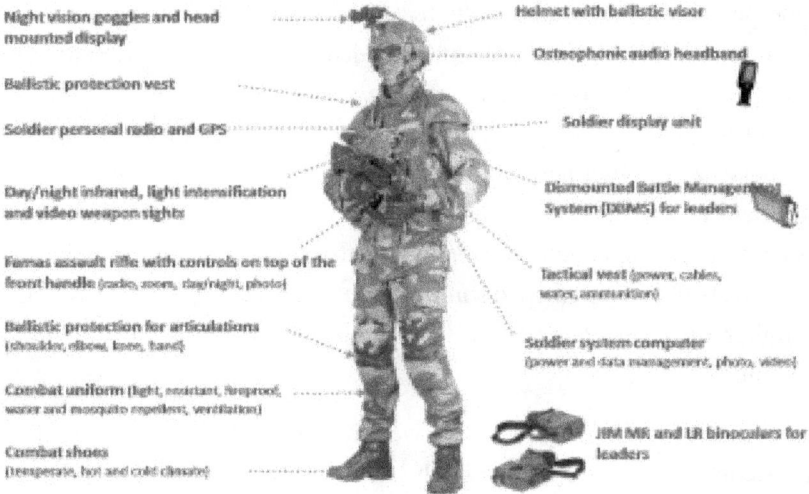

Night vision goggles and head mounted display

Ballistic protection vest

Soldier personal radio and GPS

Day/night infrared, light intensification and video weapon sights

Famas assault rifle with controls on top of the front handle (radio, zoom, day/night, photo)

Ballistic protection for articulations (shoulder, elbow, knee, hand)

Combat uniform (light, resistant, fireproof, water and mosquito repellent, ventilation)

Combat shoes (temperate, hot and cold climate)

Helmet with ballistic visor

Osteophonic audio headband

Soldier display unit

Dismounted Battle Management System (DBMS) for leaders

Tactical vest (power, cables, water, ammunition)

Soldier system computer (power and data management, photo, video)

JIM MR and LR binoculars for leaders

some kind of Christmas tree loaded with a lot of sensors, loaded with a lot of things which may impact the weight and everything. This is why I am insisting that this is the truth and as the result of more than eight years of research, including large scale trials, we decided to go for a systems approach because network revolution and digital revolution calls for systems and calls for modular solution that can be upgradable, that can be inter-operable like Gen Pathak has just explained. So we went and we decided to optimise the system for a programme length of something like 20 years because it is the length of a programme of the system and this takes into account, weight managements, energy managements and of course increase of all typical capabilities of Special Forces warriors. This is lethality, communication, mobility, ability and of course tactical awareness. So this movie will address this particular point. And I put my words into a bit more of a motion.

So moving on, what are the kinds of technologies that we were bringing to the Special Forces as of now, using the new developments that have happened over the past 15 years? Of course UAVs are critical and Sagem has been the European leader in tactical UAV and also it is now developing MALE UAVs so we have this expertise and we know that it is very important not only that the UAV should be surveying an area, but also to provide Special Forces with real time images. It is not only very important that these images should be available in the ground station of the people who monitor the UAV, the image in real time with full geo-localisation should be provided to the people on the ground to increase their capabilities. Obviously, the operational added value and the edge provided by night fighting technologies are critical. And this is also an expertise that we have developed that we have brought massively into our soldier modernisation programmes. Obviously computing and battlefield management system, we will need battlefield management systems (BMS) which are connected and which basically networked each warrior within the section, within the platoon, within the battalion and then to some other battlefield management systems, to higher up, these are very much needed to increase the collective capabilities.

And other technologies which we have brought into the programme are osteophonic technologies which basically provide warriors with the capabilities to do away with mikes; basically it is a system that allows them to speak through the bones of the skull. And this is very-very important for silence and permanent coordination within the platoon. The market is also very matured for medium altitude long range endurance UAVs, which have endurance of up to 30 hours. The UAVs can have a payload like the synthetic aperture cameras, elint, comint equipment etc. So this is very much mature and this has very much been used. For example, this one has been used in Afghanistan by the Canadian forces, Dutch forces and French forces obviously since 2003, in the frame of counter insurgency operation, including anti IED warfare.

Moving on to the soldier. Obviously what you want to do is enhance the collective and individual performance of the soldier in whatever conditions, day, night, harsh environments and sustainable conditions because generally the operations are conducted for a certain amount of time, it is not a two hours operations. In some operations such as hostage release operations it can be very short time operation, but we know that Special Forces have to cover a large span of operations in time and space. The challenge, what we are trying to do is to bring the digitisation down to the dismounted units. So like I said, everything is the question of tradeoffs. You won't find a perfect choice. The choice that was made for the French forces is the result of a trade off to satisfy the operational requirement of French forces, taking into consideration, weights, power consumption, cognitive ability, physical ergonomics and all that which is cost effective. We decided to bring a balance and we are trying the right balance between bringing into the picture the latest technology and adhering to time frame.

FELIN : a modular architecture

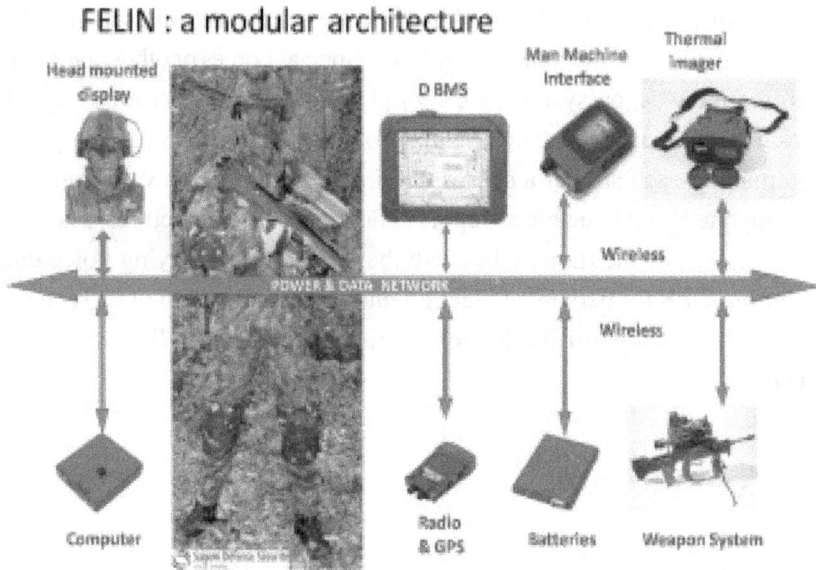

So like I said, we are trying to increase capabilities in terms of protection, utility, ability, mobility, system mobility, communication and observation. And we are doing that through a very sound optimisation of the system. The answer to the problem is that it should be modular. So you can provide a kind of sensor and weapon system along the same, transferable and cyber secure system backbone. The basic bricks that are assembled around the system back bone are the helmet mounted display, a sight for round the corner fighting solutions, dismounted battle field management system for network centric capabilities. Obviously a man machine interface. Everyone, nearly all of you, carry a smart phone. I have seen that soldiers, specifically Special Forces are very much capable of bringing into combat situations, evolved, man machine interfaces, obviously thermal imager and not uni function but multi function thermal imager and this is very much mature that allows for a complete target acquisition operation by pressing two keys. I will give you an example. If you interface within one box, the thermal imager, digital compass and GPS receiver, a laser range finder and radio channel and the laser pointer, which has six sensors in a box weighing three kilograms, let us say presently, what you do get whenever you trigger a laser range finder is, in return the information you get, it is not only the distance but you get the full geo-reference target coordinate, that can be interfaced within the system and transferred through radio to anyone who requires it, including for fire support or in the frame of Air Force Special Forces or other operations. You see the weapon system. We should be able to connect it through the back bone for around the corner fighting solution but also to transform soldiers into making each soldier a sensor within the platoon. It is very important that anyone should be able to report data, including the pictures and video footage through the radio. Obviously batteries, radio carrying voice data, including GPS for personnel location and the computer, shall be required. This is the example of the French soldier. I will not dwell upon that too much.

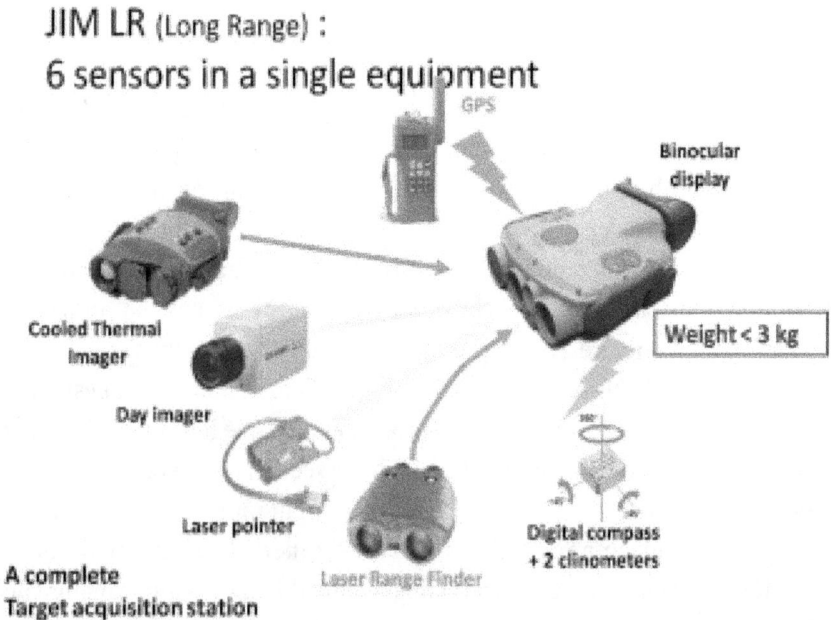

JIM LR (Long Range) :
6 sensors in a single equipment

GPS

Binocular display

Cooled Thermal Imager

Weight < 3 kg

Day imager

Laser pointer

Digital compass + 2 clinometers

A complete Target acquisition station

Laser Range Finder

So what we do is we improve the day-night capability of the soldier, indirect fighting and platoon's C^4I. This is done by providing day-night capabilities to thermal I^2 sight technologies, which are mounted on the weapon sights with two multi function binoculars and obviously two mounted night vision goggles in one sight. Some examples of how you can mount specific sights on assault rifles but also for experts on sniper rifles. Each sight embodies the configuration for the experts. For example, for the sniper, what we do generally now is that we embed it into one box, a direct optical channel, a thermal imager and a laser range finder, allowing to compress the time which it needs to acquire target and engage the target if there is an option.

Apart from thermal imagers, there are other gadgets now available. This is for example the Sagem range of products from pocket laser range finder down to the long range. Multi Function goggles are some examples of what is available in market now. There are range finders for un- cooled technology and cooled technologies. What is the main difference between both technologies? Distance of acquisition obviously and related cost which is not the same. This is what I was talking about, six sensors in single equipment which make any binocular a complete target acquisition station and not only a mere goggle. If you bring a lot of functions in, to take picture, to change the field of view, do other things, you want to still provide the soldier with a capability to engage at very short notice and this is why we are mounting these specific handle on weapon handles and providing soldiers with this capability. This is the example of the Swiss Army programme that we got awarded in 2003. You can see the handle full interface with the weapon sight. The weapon also is interfaced into this system.

Indirect fighting capability which is very important, deported vision, sector monitoring support and protection. This is an example of a man machine interface. We can also use the indirect fighting solution to the basically helmet mounted sight in this place. So the examples of helmet mounted sight on this place are very much available in the markets. Another aspect which is very important is C4I capability down to the soldier. What we wanted for the French forces is that everyone should be networked within the platoon, to increase situational awareness and in some cases to increase the continuity between mounted and dismounted troops. An example, the radio should be operable by the weapon handle to provide the capability

Indirect Fighting Solution

to the speak while the weapon is ready to engage. So it is push to talk on the weapon handle. Each radio should be capable of sending voice at that time, provide conferencing and so on. BMS, battlefield management system which provides blue force, red force tracking, a key element in the development was to select what kind of function you provide to the soldier. Obviously, a section leader, a platoon leader should not have the same capabilities as a basic warrior. So we did a lot of development to select the right functions and provide them at the right level. This is an example of how you integrate the platoon radio network within the company radio network through personal radios of the soldiers, platoon configuration for example. Before I take any question at the end of this session, I will show a little movie to put all this into motion. So it aids to extend the digitised battle space. Obviously we used UAV reconnaissance now. We can see the forces approaching the village with the UAV video available within the vehicle. Section leaders prepare the mission on the BMS through mission planning system and this is very much available and this is what we are providing to the French forces now. This is targeting through multi function binoculars, the party is getting ready to assault the village. With weapon sights and cold multi function thermal imager, comes sharing of observation set. This is very interesting. You can see this mark on the upper side. Within the vehicle, the platoon leader has decided to sign observation to the dedicated soldier. Because the un-cooled thermal imager is interfaced within the system, the orders of the platoon leader are available within the goggles of the soldier with two marks on the upper side to allow him to fix and keep his sector under observation. This is an example of what you can call a fully integrated system. We will also watch mini UAVs over the hill or over the village reconnaissance. Like I said, silent coordination through radio is very important and is done through osteo phonic headbands.

Enemy identification with weapon sight by the night, friendly force tracking, and unmanned ground vehicles are also available in the market now.There were some manufacturers providing good solutions, assault coordination through radio, these are the sniper special sights around the corner, sighting through the specific machine interface. So nobody is exposed. So it is a true around-the-corner-over-the-wall-fighting solution. So, after enemies are neutralised, soldiers will take a picture in the weapon sight and report the picture to the section leader or platoon leader. So these are the technologies available now. Weapons with specific expert sight, if required, helmet mounted night visions, multi function binoculars, any kind of electronic sensors, specific electronic vest with display with system backbone, dismounted battlefield management system, individual GPS location, video mission of UAV of ground vehicle, personal data radio, audio osteo-phone headband, the remote control handle with all kind of full ballistic protection, including NBC protection and crowd control equipment, if required.

So this will be my conclusion. As you can see, with a lot of technologies in the market, what is the key is to firstly strike the right trade off, to select the right people to absorb the technologies and Special Forces are rightly placed for that and to integrate all these technologies within a system. It is not advisable to bring each and every piece close to the soldier without a sound system integration, otherwise you may be indebted by a huge cost. A very heavy system with a cognition are going to make that which will eventually hamper mobility, communication and lethality as well as ability of the soldier.

Options for Selection of Personal Weapons and Specialist Equipment

Brigadier (Retd) Surinder Singh

The aim of my presentation in the next 15 minutes or so is designed to give you an overview of soldier modernisation technologies, highlight to you very briefly, modernisation requirements of a soldier across the full spectrum of conflict and technologies that are required to support this. I will also dwell briefly upon the Indian industrial capability to undertake this task. This was said by Lt Gen. JFC Fuller, almost 75 years back that, "99% of the battles fought in history have been won by the side using better technology" almost quarter of a century back; it is even more true today. Historically, the Indian Army had always shied away from technology, mainly because such technology was not available to us. Therefore, we wanted to compensate the lack of these technologies by stressing on other aspects of warfare which undoubtedly are equally important. Technology is advancing at very-very rapid rate today. And it will be in the interest of the Indian Armed Forces to absorb and get as much as is possible, out of this.

As a soldier, my talk is going to be at the bottom of the pyramid; that is the requirements of a soldier. A soldier requires a wide spectrum of complex technologies which he needs for target acquisition, for individual weapon, situational awareness, that includes computer, communications and things like that, protection, clothing and equipment and most important of all, power supply to sustain him throughout the operation.

Briefly covering the technology to enhance the target acquisition, we are required to enhance the soldier's sensory organ by means of optical systems in day light, image intensification in darkness and when that does not work too well, for longer ranges, thermal imagery techniques in periods of darkness and poor visibility. A soldier has to be given the means to find his own position at all times and all possible situations. He should also be able to localise or find the enemy's position. He should also be able to designate, or if not designate then at least point out the position of his targets, to the rest of his colleagues.

Very briefly about image intensification technologies, there are two parallel developments of technologies. Very often the RFP stands to mix the two together. One is the European method; the image intensifier wire tubes manufactured by Photonist or in Europe, basically follow the XD-4 type of technology which is equivalent to Gen 3 of the US. Now it is further enhanced to an XR5 tube, which is a gated tube and it gives equal performance in day as well as in night. However, this is not of any vital significance because optical sights are any day better in day time than to use any such tube. The next development is Onyx. Onyx is a development of Photonics, which is able to convert or which is able to give you a black and white picture. That is, white phosphorus is used and instead of giving the traditional green picture, it gives you a black and while clear picture. Coming to the US technologies, the most important of them is coating of the Cathode by Gallium Arsenide. This enhances the life of the tube although the magnification is reduced and also gives an equivalent picture as the XD4. So, the point that I wish to emphasise is that you cannot have both. You can either have image intensifier based on XD4 technology or you can have image intensifier based on Gallium Arsenide. Generally people tend to put everything into the requirement which is impossible to meet. Another point I wish to highlight is export restriction on the Gen 3 tubes. Anything better than that is not available for export.

Image intensifiers have a lot of problems or drawbacks. It depends upon the visibility conditions of the atmosphere; you cannot see through smoke, you cannot see when the light level is extremely low in cloudy conditions; you cannot see in dust, smoke, haze or fog. For that you have to acquire thermal imaginary techniques. It is required for longer ranges, it gives you better ranges and it gives you the ability to see through atmospheric conditions which are not conducive to transmission of light. We have both types, cooled and un-cooled thermal imaginary for both day and night operations. Un-cooled thermal imagery is advancing; the development is advancing at a very rapid rate. Today they have almost reached the threshold of detection of cooled technologies. The pictures are much better, the resolutions is much sharper and better and you almost reach a stage where you cannot only recognise but you are able to identify a particular target which was not possible in thermal imaginary till now. The limitation which is brought out by me is that you may like to use it on a sniper rifle but the resolution may not be adequate to give you an identification of the target. Particularly in counter insurgency and such roles, it may not be advisable to shoot by such a method.

Latest in the world is fusion technology. By combining the two together, you get the benefit of the positive points of both. You are able to get longer range; you are able to get a clearer picture when you fuse the two together, either by overlay or a more complex solution by digital integration or digital fusion. They are ideally suited for long range application at sniper sight but the point to remember is that they are very expensive and may be a little heavier than either of the two technologies.

Next we come to finding the main position and location of the enemy. The entire world has come to recognise Navstar constellation as the guiding force for navigation and to find own Army positions. We have to take this with a pinch of salt because particularly in Special Forces operations, the satellite signals may not be available to you, particularly when you are fighting inside buildings or inside narrow lanes and sub lanes where you need certain number of satellites to get a fix that may be denied to you, so therefore, inevitably GPS needs a back up. Also, please remember that the accuracies obtained by GPS star constellation, are coarse application, or civil application that is 30 metres for easting-northing as well as height. The precision application is not available to people who are not allies of the United States. However, our own satellite system may be able to overcome the problem, but it still needs a back up. It can fail you, you cannot really depend upon it all the time. In order to carry out navigation, if you don't have satellite signal, you definitely need a digital compass. You also need a digital compass to be able to find the direction of the enemy. A laser range finder is obviously required to get the exact range to the target; Fire control computer for accurate delivery of a grenade on the designated target. Please remember that a fire control computer is not really required for direct shooting but if you give the soldier a grenade launcher to take on targets which are defiladed from view and you want to give him air burst capability, then this requirement is important. Finally, a laser pointer which is able to direct attention of the colleague or of the rest of the squad towards the enemy that the soldier has detected. Laser designator, I would not recommend because this is a heavy item, it is required to continuously designate a target, to enable laser seeking ammunition to home on to it. So, therefore, it is not really within the purview of the individual soldier.

Coming on to the weapon, we need an integrated weapon, firing kinetic energy projectiles and also we need to give the soldier the ability to engage a target indirectly with an explosive warhead. Ideally, this would be effective provided an air burst capability is also provided to the soldier. Weapon sight, now a days, optical reflex or red dot based or laser based holo-graphics sights are available where that strict training that is required to aim is not required. I have seen a novelist, who has never handled a rifle before able to hit a target at 100 meters without firing a single round. So today technology enables the soldier to be able to aim with both his eyes open and engage a target at whatever distance. Of course this is what is applicable for shorter ranges. Now supposing you have a day time, it is not necessary to change the sight for a night sight. Today add-ons are available, it could be thermal based or it could be image intensifier based. All you need to do is clip on this sight to your day sight and you get night firing capability. One of the drawbacks is when you change a sight, you have to zero the weapon all over again. It could of course be done by means of a laser but invariably you will have to go out and fire a few rounds if you have same confidence in your weapon. You need to have a laser range finder and digital compass also to be built in into the sight. If you have all the kinds of night vision devices on the helmet and on the weapon and all over, you will have a number of displays. It will not be possible for a soldier to be able to concentrate on this. So, therefore, there is a requirement for connecting all these or integrating all these by help of blue tooth and providing the soldier with a helmet display system with which he can select the output of the sensor that he requires.

Point I would like to mention is that helmet mounted systems are still extremely expensive today and one has to think you may not be able to provide this capability to each and every soldier. Coming on to weapons you will require carbines to give an intense fire in a very short duration of time. You require GPMGs for very heavy volumes of fire, sniper rifles which are more accurate in long range in addition to the assault rifles. One of the very important facets of modern warfare is a situational awareness. A soldier must know what is around him. Up till now the soldier was under the voice control of his section commander. He really did not know what was happening in his immediate front. In order to overcome this lacuna, light weight, ruggedised touch screen computers have been set up to display digital maps, it has a capability of encrypted data and it can also transmit a video picture from any of the sensors, could also be short range or a mini or a micro UAV. You require a computer with a radio system that integrates the data transferred and management of combat oriented digital data. Computer display, organic LEDs are available which are effective even in sunlight. So anything below this probably will not be useful to the soldier because he will not be able to read the computer in day time. Technology for software already exists, ruggedised computers with display visible in bright light are available and finally a blue tooth that enables all the sensors to be integrated and to be presented to the soldier if possible, on a head up display.

Briefly about the radio coverage, for a soldier, it need not be more than about a kilometer. Nowadays we are talking about the software defined radios, IP based; there is something very interesting that is meshed topology. By the help of this meshed topology that means each radio has a built in function to transmit the transmission of one soldier across the chain. It goes without the other soldier knowing, it acts as a relay station. So these short range radios can also give you ranges of up to 9-10 kilometers very easily without coming to know or without affecting your communication. That is the way to go for shorter range communication. Of course security for transmission voice data and graphics and images are required. Now we need to take into consideration whether an individual soldier is required to be given the amount of security that is needed because he is really on the battle field itself. It doesn't matter to anybody whether somebody else is able to see that picture or not. Single band for intra-section communication, dual or multiple bands for higher communication, we have to note that all these radios have to be compatible with the FMS so that they are able to seamlessly communicate with each other.

Briefly on protection technologies. Gentlemen, there is a tendency to go in and load the weight as time passes. I would like to remind you that there are many experimental technologies that are existing today. Nano

Fibre technology is changing the scene altogether. But there is nothing available in the kitty and in the economy, required to equip every soldier with it. So, we have to do with fibre laminated technology, that is number of densely packed very fine 'Denier' fibres which provide greater protection with lower weight. So there generally has been a tendency to reduce the weight. It is a very good thing. But you have to make up your mind about the degree of protection you need and how it affects the mobility of the soldier. You cannot have one kilogram vests to be able to give you protection against 7.62 bullets. So you have to be practical about it. Many a time you find that the RFPs being issued are not achievable. People talk about liquid armour which is not rigid, which conforms to a body shape but it is still in the experiment stages. It has not found its way to India as yet, somebody may correct me if I am wrong, anywhere in the world as yet.

Coming on to the clothing and load carrying equipment, clothing is used to minimise physical strain and provide concealment. It is possible for fabric to have visual camouflage incorporated as well as thermal camouflage incorporated. CRBN is another issue. Of course it needs deliberation. You cannot have everything all the time. You require protection against kinetic energy projectiles, impact and fragments. That is well known. Some people are also talking about under vests to be fused with sensors to monitor the soldier's health and transmit this information over the radio. This is again, I feel, a luxury, may not be required or practical in the next few years. A flexible frame to fit body controls to carry ergonomically distributed loads for minimum discomfort. This is possible, it is practical and with a little imagination this can easily be achieved within the country itself. Of course all fabrics, all equipment need to be constructed with fire proof or fire retarding materials.

Ballistic helmet is an important piece of protection. We have been very reluctant to change the helmet over the years. Earlier on it was steel based then it became fibre glass but today there are materials which are lighter than Kevlar with better ballistic blast and impact protection. One of the things that comes in the way is that you have to pay more for them. Generally you would want to know why it is necessary to pay more when you can get the same protection level for a helmet which may be half a kilogram heavier. So this, it is up to the gentlemen who are serving to be able to convince the authorities that a helmet has to be light weight. I have also heard people wanting the helmet to provide protection against the 7.62 bullet. Now whatever you might do, either you make the helmet so heavy that a soldier has to take it off after about half an hour or even if the bullet strikes the neck, it will not be able to sustain the momentum. So it is not a practical decision unless there is a very revolutionary change in the protection method. Laws of physics do not permit this. Of course, visors and goggles are available with multiple filters to protect against lasers as well as fragmentation. A protection against laser is also required because you might look into the laser light by the enemy which has the potential to blind you.

And finally gentlemen, power supply. The requirement is for a soldier to operate for 96 hours with the technology available. To my mind, it is not possible unless it is supplemented by fuel technology. So, we have to take into consideration what is available and come to a very reasonable estimation of the power supply and the time a soldier is required to operate without changing it. On this line, I have just shown the expenditure on a soldier, I am not very sure if you can read it there, but I will just briefly read it out for during the World War II, this was based on US Army estimates. They spent 1981 dollars per soldier. During the South East Asian conflict, that is during the Vietnam war again, the expenditure was 1941 dollars. Now we talk about global war on terrorism. US is spending 17,452 dollars per soldier by equipping him with the sensors and the protection that is required. And futuristic people are talking about anything between 28,000 to 60000 dollars that is required to be spent on a soldier. Should you wish to give him all the gizmos that we have talked about. So this has to be kept in mind when we talk about helmet mounted displays, blue tooth connectivity, integration, network centric at the lowest level, but we have to remember the cost.

Overview of industrial capability. The private sector has been opened for defence products. With encouragement from the government, it is gearing itself for greater participation in defence sector. Unlike in the past, companies across the world are willing to share technologies with us. They are willing to co-produce. You do not really have to rely upon public sector undertakings. There is no dearth of technology that can be available to you, and private sector can provide better equipment at a lower cost. So, therefore, it is very imperative that private sector be given an opportunity in the defence market on a level playing field. Rest of the points are already on the slide that has been shown to you but what I do advocate is public sector with its formidable infrastructure in partnership with private sector with its vast reservoir of talent and resources. It can effectively accelerate the implementation of soldier modernisation programme, provided they work in harmony.

Soldier as a System- (Effectiveness Evolution)

Statistics Supplied by: Defense Manpower Data Center, Statistical Information Analysis Division (http://siadapp.dmdc.osd.mil/personnel/ CASUALTY /castop.htm)

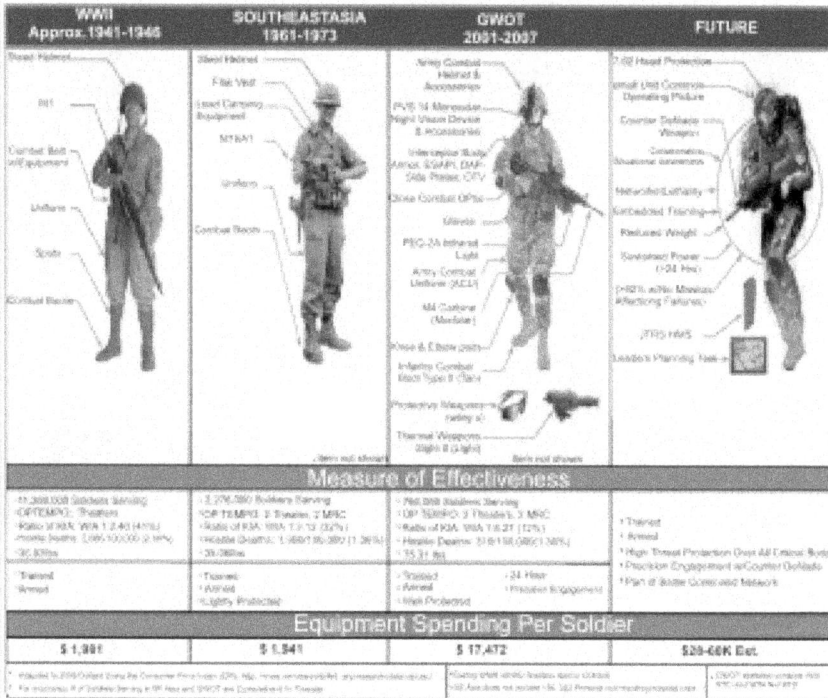

WWII Approx. 1941-1946	SOUTHEASTASIA 1961-1973	GWOT 2001-2007	FUTURE

Measure of Effectiveness

Equipment Spending Per Soldier

$ 1,981	$ 1,941	$ 17,472	$29-60K Est.

I would like to mention a couple of more technologies that are available which may be of interest to the Special Forces. One is there are radars which are available to see through the wall. So if you are confronted with the situation where the terrorists or extremists are holed up in a room, it is possible for you to know where they are, how many there are and what method you need to take. This is commonly available, it is not so rare as made out to be. It can also be done by a probe. It is possible for you to send a probe into a room which is able to transmit the information, the picture inside a room to you, to enable you to take necessary counter measures, or whatever action you need to take. With this I end my talk.

Discussion

Chairperson

I have had a very wide exposure to the modernisation aspects of the soldier as far as the Special Forces are concerned. All our speakers, they have put before us, the entire gamut of the areas which required to be modernised, what is available in the French scenario and what is available worldwide. So now the house is open. Please do identify yourself when you ask a question and who the question is addressed to. Please be brief and stick to the point.

Question: I am Baranwal, my question is for Mr. Nicolas. When you refer to soldier modernisation are you referring to future soldier programmes? And secondly, is your concept of soldier modernisation really applicable to Special Forces modernisation in Indian context?

Answer: Any system has to be modular and any requirement is specific. I have presented, demonstrated including in the frame of trial, this system or derivatives, based on the same system back bone, to a lot of forces in India, paramilitary forces including Special Forces. The feedback I have was very positive. But you are right to say that any system has to be customised to address particular requirement. This system, for example the French version was tried in France, obviously, in Guyana, tropical conditions, in Djibouti, for desert conditions and in high mountain. So we have fairly good experience and return of experience as to environment impact. However, India specific and we are more than ready, if any agency is willing to cooperate with us to customise (including DRDO) this particular system back bone in any other sensors or factors into the Indian scenario. This Felin concept is what is available as of now. The future for us was in 2003, we got the contract for system integration and applying contractual way back in 2003. So we went through a learning curve for more than 8 years. When we are talking about trade off, when we are talking about optimisation by the system, we have this 8 years experience. I will give you an example, seamless communication between weapon size and system. Yes indeed blue tooth technologies are available and they can be factored into a system. When we decided eight years ago to evaluate technologies available and what could be available 20 years down the line, prospectively, we decided that firstly there should be wire connection. Why that? Because we did not know at that time what could be the kind of jamming that you could have. Blue tooth jamming is quite easy. If you jam a blue tooth connection between the helmet mounted sight of the weapon, you kill and you destroy most of the lateral capability of the soldier. So this is one example. So you should know this system is qualified, undergoing massively in French forces and like I said, will be deployed in Afghanistan in a couple of months.

ORGANISATION STRUCTURE FOR INDIAN SPECIAL FORCES

FIFTH SESSION

Chairperson :   Lt Gen (Retd) T S Pathak

Speakers

Efficacy of Setting up a Joint   Mr Bharat Kannad, Research
SF Command   Professor, Centre for Policy
                                        Reaserch, New Delhi

Trainin g and Effective HR   Commodore R S Dhankar, Principal
Policies for Effective Management Director of Special Operations &
of SF in the Services   Diving, Indian Navy

Discussion

BIO DATA OF THE PANELISTS

Chairperson

Lt Gen (Retd) TS Pathak, AVSM, YSM and Bar, former General Officer Commanding, 1 Corps, Indian Army. He was commissioned in 1st Battalion The Parachute Regiment in June 1966 and later transferred to 9th Battalion Commandos The Parachute Regiment in July 1969. 9 Para was the first Special Forces Battalion raised by the Indian Army, post 1965.

He has Commanded 9 PARA Commandos, when the battalion was employed in provision of security cover to the Prime Minister after the assassination of Mrs. Gandhi, in Siachen Glacier and Sri-Lanka. He has been the Brigade Commander of 102 Infantry Brigade (Siachen Brigade), General Officer Commanding, 10 Infantry Division in J&K and General officer Commanding, 1Corps. His Staff tenures include Brigade Major of a Mountain Brigade in NEFA, Director Special Operations Military Operation Directorate and Chief of Staff 2 Corps.

His Instructional appointments include Instructor Class C&B at Indian Military Academy, Commander Higher Command Wing – Army War College and Commandant, National Defence College, New Delhi. The General officer was decorated with Ati Vishisht Seva Medal and Yudh Seva Medal for Service during Operations 'PAWAN', 'MEGHDOOT' and 'VIJAY'.

Speakers

Mr Bharat Karnad, Research Professor, Centre For Policy Research, New Delhi. Bharat Karnad is a Research Professor at the Centre for Policy Research, New Delhi. He is the author of India's Nuclear Policy (Praeger, 2008), Nuclear Weapons and Indian Security: The Realist Foundations of Strategy, now in its Second Edition (Macmillan India, 2005, 2002), Strategic Sellout: The India-US Nuclear Deal (Pentagon Press, 2009), and author-editor of Future Imperilled: India's Security in the 1990s and Beyond (Viking/Penguin India, 1994).

He was member of the (First) National Security Advisor Board, National Security Council, Government of India and member, of the nuclear doctrine drafting group and, formerly, Adviser on Defence Expenditure to the (Tenth) Finance Commission, India. He has been a Visiting Scholar at Princeton University and the University of Pennsylvania, and at international think tanks, such as the Shanghai Institutes of International Studies and the Henry L. Stimson Center, Washington, DC, and is regular lecturer at Indian military training forums and institutions.

Commodore RS Dhankhar, Principal Director of Special Operations & Diving, Indian Navy. He is an alumnus of National Defence Academy, DSSC Wellington and College of Naval Warfare, Karanja. He was commissioned on 01 Jul 82 and qualified as a Marine Commando (MARCO) in Feb 87, which was followed by deployments in Sri Lanka with 1st Para Commandos & 10 Para Commandos. He headed the MARCO Team, instrumental in intervention of 'MV Progress Light' during OP CACTUS.

As a young Lt Cdr, he raised MARCOS (East) based near Vishakhapatnam in Nov 92; followed by a tenure as Staff Officer (Special Operations) in Western Naval Command and as Deputy Director and Director, duties in Special Operations & Diving Directorate at Naval HQ.

Presently, the Commodore is the Principal Director of Special Operations & Diving, since 31 Dec 09.

His other non SF appointments include Command of INS Bedi, INS Dunagiri and INS Ganga. The Commodore was Naval Component Cdr and Chief Staff Officer (Operations) in the only Joint Command of Andaman & Nicobar.

OPENING REMARKS

Lt Gen (Retd) TS Pathak, AVSM, YSM and Bar

We have gone through the last session about modernisation aspects and as I said in the last session - structures are very important. Aspects, concepts and technology are fine, but structures are the things that are going to deliver. Along with that, we will be addressing the issue of human resource (HR) aspects, during the session. I hand over to Mr Bharat Karnad, who will be talking about the issues of structures.

Efficacy of Setting Up a Joint SF Command

Mr Bharat Kannad

I am known for the slight bit of work I have done for the nuclear policy field. Fewer people know me for some little bit of work I have done for conventional military field. I am particularly proud of the report I did for the 10th Finance Commission, wherein, I was tasked with the re-prioritising of Defence Expenditure Programmes. This was the 10th Finance Commission and we submitted the report in end 1994, which is almost 20 years since I started writing the report. The recommendations of the report were completely accepted by the Indian government. My recommendations were- because conflicts were not going to be of the kind of military mass on military mass, kind of things of the older era, you have to build up Special Forces for expeditionary, counter insurgency and other tasks. I had advocated then, in the report, Special Forces Command, a joint command, incorporating all the Special Forces of all the military services. I did not then consider that every police force, every constabulary will have its commando element and regard themselves as Special Forces. Because, there is such a proliferation, we should restrict our ambit to military field simply because, otherwise you get into the confusion of Ministry of Home Affairs and everybody else tries to get into the field, as far as command and control is concerned, of these kind of forces. This, by the way, in a sense, establishes my modest credentials in the Special Forces field. As I have heard a galaxy of renowned commanders of Special Forces from India and abroad, I think I feel a little daunted to speak about Special Forces.

The antecedents of Special Forces in the Indian context are really remarkable. India, perhaps, not known to many, has suffered at the hands of Special Forces actions. Starting with, if I may say so, just to remind people, that it was Robert Clives' campaign against the Nawab of Arcot that really began the great colonial enterprise that ended up being the British Raj in India. They were Special Forces basically because Clive went with just 30 British officers and some 150 odd people from the Chennai area, Madras Presidency. In the Special Forces, the need for a joint forces command is in one sense just too obvious to belabour. The most immediate thing that can be said as to the need for a Special Forces command is that it is invariably worked in war. And indeed when wars are started, major wars have happened in the past, the supreme commanders have ended up grouping Special Forces for more efficient and effective use, in terms of realising outcomes. This happened for instance with Eisenhower, where after the initial years, separate Special Forces like the special operations executive in Britain, SES in Britain, and the SPS and OSS in United State Service were grouped together by Eisenhower in his headquarters' group where there was one controlling authority that controlled all Special Forces operations. After the initial few years in Second World War this became a greater success in terms of Special Forces actions. In the South East Command, again it is not generally known, Mountbatten had the largest number of Special Forces under command. More than the Supreme Commander in Europe - as Mountbatten under South East Asia Command headquartered in Kandy, had a multitude of Special Forces working against the axis power.

Now with this kind of past, it is really ironic that the great Indian Army, began losing that Special Forces edge, with independence. First of all, we demobilised two air borne divisions which we had in 1947. We were one of the five countries in the world, with the power projection capability - one of the five. We demobilised it for a better reason that we followed the model or the examples set by the British Army. This was in part because our Cols who were ramped to Generals overnight simply didn't have strategic sense. That is one conclusion we can come to. It is an obvious conclusion and that is the only conclusion. Because they were unit commanders at most in the Second World War. Suddenly they are presented with the Command of an Army and don't realise adequately, the primacy of Special Forces, leave alone the necessity of jointness in the use.

The friction between conventional military, regular units and Special Forces are well known. And this is true all over the world. Indeed Major David Sterling, the legendary unit commander of the SAS in the Long Range Desert Group said somewhere that "he fought as many battles with the military headquarters as with the axis powers". In other words, there has always been an ill-fitting relationship between conventional military and the Special Forces and it is nothing new. Now the question is whether one can work around the obvious kinds of bureaucratic hurdles. When the Special Forces were first set up certainly, in the OSS, for instance (and it may be true as well, Gen Lamb perhaps will confirm otherwise), the people who were considered mis-fits and officers and personnel with discipline issues, were dumped by regular units into the Special Forces. It is precisely the kind of personal initiative, risk taking etc. all the attributes the Special Forces are known for, that cannot be maintained if these come under the separate military commands. Meaning, if it is conventional military that controls the Special Forces, you, first of all, have the real problem, as you all know, of lack of appreciation or what it is you have in terms of the instrument. This may be for bureaucratic or other reasons; or simply because you have to share the budget.

In the Indian setting, I think that was the first, if I recall and I tried to confirm it with Gen Lidder earlier in the day, the first attempt and trying to have some kind of a separate Special Forces identity and then institutionalise it. It was somewhere in the late 1980s when the then Col Rustam Nanavati produced a proposal for making PARA the nucleus for the Special Forces contingent controlled by the MO Directorate, Army Headquarters. That was shot down, or rather it didn't go very far, because the then Western Army Commander and earlier the ADG, MO, Lt Gen VK Nayyar himself being the Commanded 5 PARA in the past and being the Colonel Commandant of the Parachute Regiment, nixed it for the reason, as he put it in his memoirs, I have just read his memoirs that he sent to me to read over the weekend, so it is fresh in my memory. He says that the reason I opposed it was, first of all because the Indian Army follows the regimental system, the question of treatment of widows and so on, who become in-charges of those responsibilities.

Well, okay, the second, more substantive reason, he put forward in the Army Commanders' Conference at that time was that you cannot have a separate Special Forces even if it is controlled by the MO directorate, if in war these Special Forces have to then adhere to command plans. It seems reasonable. And that's precisely the reason why yesterday I brought up the subject when Gen Lidder mentioned that and I think it is a very feasible and excellent proposal, to make the NSA, the person heading a separate Special Forces grouping command, whatever you may call it. Just to refresh your memory about what Gen Lidder said, in peace time operations, whatever clandestine actions are required can be done with the NSA in command, and as soon as there is war and mobilisation for war, the Special Forces revert to their respective theatre commands or whatever. Which is precisely the problem, because they go back to being treated as a tactical adjunct to the army plans. Exactly the reason why earlier we have heard our Special Forces not having any strategic purpose at all, in terms of the usage and utility and in terms of outcomes. You have to merely analyse the record of the really decisive Special Forces actions in the world and they have been remarkable actions. Yesterday, again I think Gen Lidder mentioned about the Special Forces action against the Nosk-hydro in Norway to deny Hitlerite Germany, the heavy water for the weapons programme. That is the kind of decisive action that couldn't have been taken. This was, by the way, in the latter part of the Second World War and was managed by the headquarters group in Eisenhower's command. It is a sort of thing, I think, that confirms and reinforces the need for joint forces to be grouped under separate command and does not play around too much having them to revert to the services, the conventional militaries because that defeats the purpose and blunts the edge. Yesterday the French representative mentioned coherence and that really is at the heart of the matter. Special Forces, whatever their service backgrounds, once they become Special Forces and I would like to call it Special Operations Command really, rather than Special Forces, the problem is what you call them also matters, Special Forces is now, in a sense, the term that has expropriated within the conventional military usage and therefore, it gets co-opted. I rather think of it as a Special Operations Forces Command and give it a slightly different identity altogether rather than what we have been essentially playing around with, over the last 40 odd years.

A joint forces command ensures economy of effect, economy in the employment of resources. Because there is a unitary command it knows what it wants and what is needed for any operation to fulfil and realise whatever missions are tasked to them. They are best judges in terms of acquisition and as we heard earlier, some of the problems of fast track acquisition etc. happen because of the usual bureaucratic logjam and the very normal gumming up of words that the bureaucrats are prone to do. Special Forces command, a singular command, should that come into being, will have tactical expertise to design, shape their capabilities in the best manner possible. This is because they are used to working within terrain specific various resources, specific milieu and so to task the planning and for ultimate okaying by some service headquarters or somebody else in the Ministry of Defence, I would think, it would undermine the utility and the effectiveness of Special Forces.

I have said this in my confidential report about getting the best people for the special forces. I had a talk on the sidelines with Gen Eizenberg of Israeli forces. By procedure and norms, the Israelis and because it is a compulsory service, every citizen has to go through military service, so they are in a very different boat than we are, the fact of the matter is that after the fighter pilot, because not everybody can fly or has the skills to fly, the Special Forces get the best talent. The third in order are the submarine arm and then the land forces etc. That perhaps Israel can afford and manage because it is a forced conscript Army. In terms of the Indian system how do you get the best talent? I think this is where I also remember stressing the reward structures. Gen Lamb told me last evening that the SAS appointment does not, any more, carry as much weight as it once did. I don't know what the reasons are, but until about 10 years ago, unless you had a SAS or an SBS posting on your record, you could not get on to Gen Staff ranks or rather you missed out on points. You could still have become Flag officer but it would be a bit more difficult. We have to again begin thinking, of course in such a vast army of 1.3 million, perhaps that is not possible, but those who chose to come into special service should be amply rewarded and that should be the incentive; someone earlier mentioned you know, entrant level corporate salaries at 1 lac or whatever.

There is a general dismay that you hear and, Chairman, I will end on the score, that somehow the incoming manpower is not as good etc. I tend to disagree, I disagree because the incoming officers that I find, when I go to IMA and so on and so forth, are perhaps even better motivated. They may not have the social graces that some of us may wish they had, but that be damned, if they are not highly motivated and it can't be used for purposes that we need to in the military sphere. But in the more material aspects of rewards and remunerations, there are special allowances etc. and I am not quite sure what the extent is, I should have touched on these points with Gen Pathak, before I spoke. So maybe I am off base here. But unless the Special Forces' officers and men get a substantial and significant increase in their remuneration packages, to add on to the motivational aspects, self motivational aspects, because it is adventurous, because it is risk taking etc., I mean some people thrive on it, it will not work. Again from the SAS example, I am told that generally on average, SAS persons pulls down 2/3rds more salary in terms of their remuneration package than a counterpart serving in infantry or mechanised or armoured regiments. Some such reward systems and remuneration system have to be built in if you are going to attract the very motivated, risk taking people that you want. And in some sense then, something like a Joint Special Operations Forces Command would help, will have enough political clout, much more than if it were a mere part of Army Headquarter, some cell there, working to further the SF cause or within the Navy or within the Air Force and to have these all amalgamated with the separate skill sets.

And one last thing I should mention, I looked at the skill sets and this is in the public domain of the United States, we don't quite reveal everything of our Special Forces, so I won't say much but in the US Special Forces' scheme of things, there are almost as many as 120 skill sets and I was doing a rough arithmetic on the kind of skill sets we have. I am afraid, without going into numbers, they are a lot fewer. This, I think, hurts the versatility of Special Forces, which is one of its hallmark because only cross train in so many disciplines, I cannot go through the whole, I mean 120 odd assuming, that's the maximum figure one tries to ideally aim at achieving, this again is something a Special Forces, Special Operations Forces Command will help realise.

I fwish to mention one thing, perhaps of some interest to you because it is in my field of interest, is what I call a nuclear commando simply because I think you are going to see situations developing in the neighbourhood where we would need special operation forces who are capable of inserting themselves into Pakistan or somewhere where there is a loose nuke kind of a contingency, or the possibility where nuclear materials for radiation diffusion devices have been leaked to some extremist elements for these to be intercepted or that particular option to be pre empted etc. and that is a specialised task. It really cannot be done by the normal SF. It will require specially trained teams like the Americans have Nuclear Explosion Teams (NEXT), that are already there, actually in Pakistan, trying to map and locate their nuclear assets and in the contingencies, trying to neutralise them. We should, I think, seriously look to having such a unit, but it will have to be all officers, is what I think, in terms of the kind of capability and intellect, because they will be handling complex technologies for detection and for neutralisation, be it weapons or the nuclear material etc., it will be an all officer kind of outfit where you will have to build in the adequate reward structure and so on. I am not quite sure how it will work out in practical terms, but there is such a need. This should have to marry up with the kind of language skills, whether in Pashto or Sindhi or something because one thing is clear in terms of being able to operate best in the milieu like Pakistan. Israelis or the Americans and all the rest of that caboodle is going to be identified very fast on the ground. Indians have the obvious advantage if only we build up the skill sets to deal with the contingencies, simply because we are in the frontline, those countries are not.

Training and Human Resource Policies for Effective Management of Special Forces in the Services

Commodore R S Dhankar

Gentlemen, by now we are very well updated, rather saturated, with various issues confronting Special Forces. In the course of my talk on Special Forces Training and HR issues, I will try to bring out, in front of this august audience, certain aspects which the Indian Defence Special Forces are presently faced with and recommend measures for effective management of Special Forces training and HR policies in the services.

It is said that those who do not learn from their past mistakes are doomed to repeat them. The present state of management of training and HR issue of the Special Forces in the three services can be equated to the state of US Special Forces in early 1980s. Because of the failure of hostage rescue mission from Iran in 1980 and unnecessary casualties suffered during operation 'Urgent Fury' in Grenada in 1983, the then US Defence Secretary Mr Weinberger and Mr Noel Koch, a Pentagon official, had turned the heat on service headquarters to revitalise their Special Forces. However, from the start of the Special Forces revitalisation programme, the Service headquarters were not fully behind the effort.

With few opportunities for the Special Forces, to convince the military skeptics of their worth, revitalisation continued to lurch forward. For Noel Koch, the job of persuading the military to carry out the policies of the administration had proved lonely and frustrating. He found himself unable to force the powerful bureaucracy in the Pentagon to move at anything like the speed demanded by Weinberger. Mr. Koch, during his testimony before Appropriations Committee on 10 Apr 1984, had stated "Human nature resists change and the case at hand is no exception. And, of course, when defence policy changes, defence budgets also change and anytime one reallocates resources, vested interests and status quo are challenged". Koch went on to set out four main areas of concern that were still unresolved, even after four years of revitalisation efforts.

As Special Forces will be among the first to be sent to war, they have to be at a constant high state of readiness. Yet, Koch pointed out, the strength of the Army's special forces groups was 12 percent below authorised wartime requirements; also, although all groups should have been at the highest readiness, in fact to ensure that Special Forces trainees reach desired level of (ALO-2) training, standards were lowered, thus artificially improving the ratings.

Special Forces typically require small quantities of specialist equipment not in service with other units. The procurement system was not capable of handling such items and the flow of new equipment to the Special Forces was very low. For example, in perhaps extreme case of the PRC-70 radio, it took seventeen years from the day it was ordered, for it to be delivered to the special operations forces, for which it was intended. By that time, it was already some ten years out of date. The experience of our Special Forces in all three services has not been very different from the above, in trying to induct specialist equipment.

In the early days of the Green Berets, many recruits came from Eastern European countries that had been taken over by the communists. It was common for each A-Team to have half of the team fluent in another language, often their mother tongue. However, that source of recruits dried up, in 1984, the predominant language, other than English was Spanish. But, in the regions of the Third World, in which other languages predominate, US could deploy no more than one fully language qualified 12-man Special Forces detachment to defend its interests. Indian Defence Special Forces also need to bolster this capability to desired levels.

Special Forces have traditionally been the graveyard for a service career. In the past, no officer with a career in the Special Forces has been promoted beyond brigadier, and even that rank is very rare. As a result, ambitious officers stay in Special Forces for only a short time. Koch told the subcommittee, "If we are to attract and retain the highly qualified personnel we need for special operations, their career opportunities must be comparable to those of their peers in other branches of military service".

Special Forces personnel undergo a careful selection process and mission specific training beyond basic military skills to achieve entry-level special operations skills. These programmes make unlikely any rapid replacement or generation of Special Forces personnel or capabilities. Detailed intelligence and knowledge of the culture(s) and language(s) of the areas where the mission is to be conducted is a must. Rigorous individual, collective and operational training, followed by rehearsals of the mission are integral to the conduct of all special operations. There are four cardinal universal truths as far as effective management of training and HR issues of Special Forces is concerned. From the previous US Special Forces' examples highlighted by me and as we go along with the presentation, it will be evidently clear why they are so important.

Training Management. It needs to be understood that Special Forces cannot be mass-produced like conventional forces. Any rapid expansion of Special Forces would almost certainly undermine this proven selection and training process. The Special Forces community would be forced to cut corners and lower standards in order to produce more Special Forces personnel. The results would be a degraded operational capability and tragically, a greater probability of mission failure and lost lives. And while we might garner a certain sense of satisfaction with more Special Forces teams on the books, it would be a hollow one at best. In our haste to build up adequate Special Forces Para Bns have been converted to Para Special Forces Bns, in my view it would have resulted in compromising of standards. In the mid 1960s, the 22 SAS had to ward off pressures, of their being subsumed by the Para Regiment. In 1987, a wartime SAS veteran, Col David Sutherland, published a paper stating that "they (The Para officers) began a series of manoeuvres, to group 22 SAS with the Parachute Regiment, in some form of general airborne formation in which, by some force of numbers, they would be dominant partners".

Most of the professional Special Forces in the world are capable and are achieving the desired results because they have been very selective about the type of individuals they bring into these organisations. After the initial screening, during which a trainee's self discipline, motivation, physical and mental toughness, sharpness of mind and observation powers are tested, emphasis is laid on skill development to enable his flexibility of employment, in small teams, for varied tasks under different environmental conditions. On an average, the attrition rate for selection of Special Forces, world over, hovers around 70 percent with yet another 10-15 percent of the balance lost in the ensuing Special Forces Qualification Course.

This is not attrition for attrition's sake; in fact, the trainees are not harassed, hazed, or otherwise coerced into quitting at any time. Rather, the physical and mental rigours of the training, cull out those who do not possess the necessary attributes for service in Special Forces. The end result is Special Forces personnel, who are tough, self-reliant, innovative, and flexible.In his study of military Elites, Roger Beaumont argues that Special Forces tend to suffer from what he calls the selection – destruction cycle. The most able volunteers are selected for most hazardous missions and suffer casualties more than other units, as a result.

Recruiting and training Special Forces personnel is a time consuming process. It invariably takes about three years to get a Special Forces recruit up to a basic level of competence and then another few years in the field before such men are ready for anything serious. Each member of Special Forces is expected to be competent in a wide range of skills, such as small arms, field craft, demolition, communication, navigation, first aid, unarmed combat and survival techniques. This is followed by further continuation or advanced training in various methods of clandestine insertion/extraction, methods by air, land, sea and underwater. Regional orientation and language training is a time consuming and protracted process.

The training methodology of Indian Special Forces, common to all three services, has more or less been the age old tradition of practical training and common sense. Today, if we observe, our Special Forces are still equipped, primarily, at the personal level of weapons and gears such as reliable body armour, good load bearing combat kit, NVDs etc. Accordingly, their existing training level concentrates on building endurance, honing basic skills and developing/practicing tactics, mainly for Direct Action missions.

In order to augment the existing capability of our Special Forces, more specialised gear such as Special Operations satellite based communication equipment, giving the Special Forces operators instant message capabilities, specialised platforms for mobility in operational area such as fast boats, all terrain vehicles, need to be inducted. Discreet launch and recovery platforms such as Midgets, Special Operations Vehicles, Heavy Lift Helicopters, Long Range Transport Aircrafts are still a long way from the inventory of our Special Forces personnel and therefore the development of training and tactics on these equipment is lacking. These platforms need to become part of daily workup and training routine of Special Forces for effective man-machine integration.

It is said, train as you fight and fight as you train. Any Special Forces personnel in addition to his physical strength and endurance, also requires possessing extraordinary level of skills and psychic profiles to be successful. The psychic or intuitive profiles of the Special Forces soldier can be only developed if they are continuously trained and deployed in the circumstances they are required to perform. In wartime, Special Forces men should expect to be isolated and surrounded by enemy forces as part of their working environment. To illustrate this, an exchange of message between SAS Patrol during Gulf War 1991 and their forward HQs goes like this-SAS Patrol-Surrounded from all sides by enemy divisions...Forward HQ-Good, you are obviously in the right place.

Therefore, sustained small team operations training under hostile conditions is a prerequisite for development of such profiles. In order to avoid overstretch by deployment on routine tasks and to maintain the 'Special' edge of these forces, it is essential that the Special Forces follow a 'Three Team Cycle' concept i.e. training, operations and administration. This three team concept ensures that the Special Forces are continuously trained to hone their skills, and yet ready for operations without combat fatigue.

Human Resource Management. Humans are more important than hardware. In order to train, individuals need to be selected. What kind of men want to get selected as Special Forces? Why would a young sailor comfortably settled in his parent branch of Navy, volunteer to serve in Special Forces that requires tremendous personal investment and sacrifice? High pay is generally not the clear answer as there are several other branches which provide with equally good remunerations if not better.

Each volunteer's motivation is different. The initial stimulus may be nothing more than adrenaline addiction. Some strongly believe in giving their best to their country for personal patriotic reasons; others view Special Forces service as the ultimate test for determining whether they had "the right stuff"; still others value the esteem with which their being a commando is seen by the general public. The sense of being elite is quite intoxicating, especially in the youth. (As we know, a Special Forces person, decked out in full uniform with his badges and unit emblem proudly displayed, tends to attract attention and admiration from the general public). In order to get selected and undergo the most demanding physical and mental gruelling, one must have belief in self because " Life's battles don't always go to the stronger or faster men, but sooner or later the man who wins, is the man who thinks he can". The endeavour of Special Forces selectors and trainers is to remain on the look out for such men of character and skill.

It is a well known fact that JCOs form the backbone of any good military unit. However, at least half of the Special Forces personnel recruited, are lost within the five years of their full capability because of loss of motivation attributed to increased combat duties, injuries, lack of promotion prospects and the opportunities offered in the civil street. A Para Special Forces soldier profile would be similar to a MARCOS profile in the Navy. A sailor joins Navy at roughly 18-20 yrs of age and needs at least 2 years to learn the basic skills required to serve in the Navy. Then he undergoes almost 2 years of training to qualify as a Special Forces man. It takes another 2 years of combat exposure, specialised training, interaction with other Special Forces and higher qualification examinations before he is fully groomed into an effective operator. So, finally after 6 years of his service, he becomes a reliable and dependable Special Forces operator who can be part of a team to deliver results with little fear of failure. And this, when presuming that the sailor will opt for Special Forces immediately on the first available opportunity. A sailor would have an option to leave service after 15 years and thus for the last 2 years, he invariably moves out of the operational unit to prepare for the outside world.

Therefore it will be seen that, despite all the investment in terms of training and experience, all that has been achieved is just 7 years of service as a reliable Special Forces operator who can undertake serious operations. Considering that there are little incentives for the experienced Special Forces man to continue, the brighter ones who meet the high standards confidently join the civil street, and the others with less desire to experiment continue and rise in the Special Forces organisation. Ideally we would like to retain the talent, but it's hard to convince or stop Special Forces personnel who voluntarily joined the force and endured the additional effort, stress and danger to become a Special Forces operator.

As far as officers are concerned, in the higher echelons of the services, a traditional skepticism about Special Forces exists. Their elitism, independence, apparent informality and special role, out of mainstream operations in large-scale warfare, all make them a class apart. This factor can act as an intangible blocking mechanism to officers' later promotion. In August 1985, Dan Daniel, the chairman of the US, House Armed Forces Readiness Committee, had suggested that Special Forces have always been peripheral to the philosophical core of the military. They have historically been the target of mistrust and suspicion and their capabilities and requirements are poorly understood. If they are to become truly effective, they must have their own intellectual and professional core around which they can coalesce and mature.

Recommendations. Presently each service is separately carrying out training and education of their Special Forces in service specific tasks. This training is conducted in their respective schools and partially through inter-service Special Forces institutions. It would be an ideal situation if a joint Special Forces structure is evolved and put in place as most of the advanced and practicing Special Forces nations have already done. However, considering the present politico-military constraints, a beginning can be made by adopting interim measures in small steps.

Undertake comprehensive study of the existing Special Forces training structure and methodology in the three services and indentify areas of common skills development such as communication, navigation, marksmanship, field-craft, basic parachuting, survival and ISR techniques.

Start conducting basic training for all three service volunteers, including officers, together in order to strengthen inter service camaraderie and encourage jointmanship. The benefits of this joint training will far outweigh initial investment in terms of time and resources.

The basic training can be followed up by individual service specific training with a focus on their core competencies. Thereafter, the advanced joint training capsules need to be indentified and worked out both for ORs, JCOs and officers and responsibilities assigned to suitable service headquarters for conduct of specialised joint training such as leadership, language, intelligence, weapon maintenance, EOD, diving and CFF courses.

The focus of the training should shift to enable small Special Forces teams' survival and sustenance and operations in hostile conditions. The composition of these teams should invariably remain below eight personnel, where each member is an expert of one primary skill and is cross trained for a secondary skill (Communication, Demolition, Medicine, and Weapons/sniper). The ability to launch and recover these small teams by support platforms and the associated training to do so need to be augmented in a time bound manner.

Presently, the Army and Navy draw volunteers for their Special Forces units from the already recruited manpower; whereas Air Force has started direct recruitment from the civil street. Both have their advantages and disadvantages which need to be studied in detail vis-a-vis the practices existing in advanced nations and work out a model suited to Indian Special Forces. In the interim period, measures to retain the highly qualified and vertically specialised Special Forces personnel, need to be adopted.

Get the right guys. If required introduce psychological/scientific screening methods during the selection process. The psychologists (who test SAS recruits) look for those who, on the test, are above average in intelligence; assertive; happy-go-lucky; self-sufficient; not extremely intro- or extrovertish. They do not want people who are emotionally unstable; instead they want forthright individuals who are hard to fool and not dependent on orders.

As brought out earlier, in the higher echelons of military service, it has become common to deride the capabilities of Special Forces and deflate their ego, which results in conflict of cultures - the one dedicated to intellectual abstraction and the other expressing itself by action rather than talk. There is a need to bridge this gap and encourage their elitism.

In the advanced nations, if a useful Special Forces operator decides to stay in service beyond his mandatory tenure, he is offered certain incentives in terms of pay packets/free education for children etc. There is a need to look at the terms and conditions for introduction of similar incentives for retention of experienced and talented Special Forces personnel.

The promotion prospects, both for the men and officers, need to be improved. In the worst of times, Special Forces service has been a career - killer, which means that those who choose to stick, must do so out of pure dedication. If we are to develop true Special Forces professionalism, the three services must reward the services of their Special Forces personnel in an equitable way.

The defence establishment of India is still floundering in its attempts to raise a force which could be truly termed as Special Force, as commonly understood or defined. The art of managing Special Forces is learnt over a period of time by gaining experience of their utilisation, during various contingencies, especially unconventional ones. In order to give them proper Special Forces edge, there is a pressing need to induct state of the art equipment within the Special Forces of three services, especially launch and recovery platforms. On completion of individual training, Special Forces personnel have to become adept at exploitation of high-tech equipment and develop confidence in use of launch and recovery platforms.

In conclusion, I would like to say that the governing principles of Special Forces truths, i.e. Special Forces cannot be mass produced, competent Special Forces cannot be raised post emergency, quality is better than quantity and humans are more important than hardware, should not be lost sight of, whilst trying to manage training and HR policies of Special Forces of our services.

Discussion

Chairman

Question: I am Squadron Leader Ravi, I am looking after Garud from Air Headquarters. My question pertains to my paper which is put forth by Lt Gen Chandrashekhar, retired of course, who says that Special Forces need to look at a new set of skills. In the emerging net centric warfare scenario, what are the kind of new skills that you would envisage the Special Forces to look into?

Answer (Gen T S Pathak): Talking about the net centric warfare, you are talking about what special skills are required. The way I look at it is that the net centric warfare is based on technology, which is just a tool. We want a person to be aware of the environment, appreciate the correct course of action, a capability, that is what you develop. It is not a skill, it is a capability that you have got to develop. That comes with the exposure and that comes with the experience. The other side is we talk about net centric warfare. I don't think today a country has a platform or experimented with the tools that are there. We are looking at presentations and forming ideas. Once you experience it, everything doesn't run as per the presentations that were shown. There are glitches. The manufacturer is not showing you the glitches. Once you experience it, you will carry out the mid course corrections. That's all I have.

Question: I just wish to make one small comment. After the things that I have heard, some things were said about the conversion of battalions and raising of battalions and other stuff like that. Sir, what I want to speak on this issue is that what has gone under the bridge has gone under the bridge. I think we need to realise that and we have a situation here where a number of SF battalions have been raised and they will find their footing in the near future because I feel that they are equally bright and it will take them some time. I think the greatest challenge that we need to focus on and also the think tanks, that is the Generals that they need to portray is firstly to find us the right mandate. Presently we have the same mandate and the same tasking and we are used in the similar manner as infantry. There are no different parameters; hence we lose our respect. What we need to do is have a different tasking, we need to look outwards. Do we have the political will or the military will to do that? Do we have the will to create a Special Operations Command in which we will have the SF, air borne, who will undertake special operation? They need to be part of it, the NSG, the Marcos and everybody. I think that is the issue which should be troubling us than the small issues of battalion converting or battalion which has to be raised. I think, sir in due course of time, everybody will reach the same level.

Answer (Gen Pathak): I just want to mention a few things before I pass on the mike. The point is yes, what has happened has happened. You cannot put the clock back. But what has been emphasised is that we are not even trying to put the clock back here. When we were talking about mandates, this is what Mr. Bharat Karnad said, let's look at a Joint Special Operations Command, slight distinction from a Joint Special Forces Command. This is one part of it. The thrust has been - let's club all together to optimise and maximise training and equipment. That's what we are talking about and that's exactly what you said, you were looking at. Other aspect the mandate will come, the political will can come without your asking for it. Just remember that, this is a country which has exhibited very hard options in time in earlier years. So let's not bother too much about the political will. It is a question of organisation, structure and capabilities. Once the challenge is there, the political will, will be there. But capacity, capability building takes a long time. That is what we should address.

Commodore Dhankar: See that point was made on conversion and raising, to emphasise the point that SF forces cannot be mass produced. So that was the point that has been emphasised. Now, about our suggestions on training. Suggestions which I have made, that is basic training and advanced training, if we put them through, obviously their standards will come up. But we have to put them through. The main distinction between Special Forces and the general thing, I feel is, that the point which we have been harping on is about small team operations, where people are individualist in the teams of four or eight, they are left behind somewhere in very difficult circumstances, they should be able to take their own decision and act rather than look up at the platoon or company commander or asking him what to do. That conventional thinking has to be broken and individualistic thinking has to be brought into mind. That is the main thing. That unconventional part has to come into them.

Gen Pathak: Another aspect of lot of water flown and you cannot put the clock back. But definitely an effort must be made to enlarge your intake base. Instead of limiting that intake base to one regimental centre, to improve your quality and enlarge your intake base from all over the Army; that is the thing that need a bit of reforms. That's my view. You can take your call.

Question: I fully agree with your comment of enlarging the intake base. I am Major Santosh from 21 PARA. The present recruitment process for the men of Parachute Regiment is, I feel, though it has lived the test of time but we have scope of improvement. Firstly, we don't have volunteers. What we have presently are the personnel who want to join and do service and they are put through the Parachute Regiment Training Centre and then inducted into the unit, though after some probation and selection, they go through the selection procedure. However, we need to convert this Parachute Regiment Training Centre into a Parachute Regiment Selection Centre. Instead of recruiting the individuals straight from the civil street, we need to take personnel from the Armed Services volunteers and then laterally select them and then induct them into the units. I feel this would be a more prudent way of selecting volunteers than recruiting people from civil street and then training them to become Special Forces soldier.

Answer: I think the Indian Army Special Forces are, may be the few in the world that their intake is based on a recruit with just a basic training and then he comes into the service. The aim of recruit training is for the guy to take his position in a rifle section. Now, in those 52 weeks from a raw person, you are training him to take his position in a Special Forces battalion, I think there is something wrong. Logically, people who have got about 2-3 years of service, volunteer and when you select and train them, I think that would be a better foundation to build it in. If I recall, I totally agree with you on what you have said.

Chairman's Concluding Remarks

Chairperson

To summarise, I thank both the panelists on their thought provoking presentations. I just want to highlight two points of what Mr. Bharat Karnad said about a Joint Special Operations Command. It has got an entirely different connotation, dive a little deeper, as far as Joint Forces Command, Special Forces Command has got a different connotation, can have different connotations than a Joint Special Operation Command, that is one aspect of it. Ponder over it. The other is what Commander Dhankar said about HR management. Well, in a lighter vein, I will say promotion prospects in the Army, I don't think, are so bad because of one battalion that is 9 PARA, three of us Generals sitting over here, so possibly it can't be so bad, but definitely HR management does require a lot of serious thought.

CLOSING REMARKS

LT GEN (RETD) AS KALKAT, SYSM, PVSM, AVSM, VSM

It has been one and a half day of the most interesting, highly cerebral and over objective discussion on a subject which is very dear to the hearts of many of you here and also personally to me. We were honoured today and yesterday by having distinguished visitors from abroad, which enabled us to see how they practice this. And the fact that the who's who were here from abroad and have participated on the ground. We can all read books; we can all have professionals to talk from abroad. They are very good. But we were fortunate here to have people who have actually handled the soldiers on ground in battle situations. It is a rare opportunity to hear these visitors from abroad.

As far as Special Forces are concerned, as I said, it is dear to my heart too. I go back a little bit. The first time, the three Special Forces battalions got together in the operations and were launched, was in Sri Lanka where I had the honour of commanding the force. They were part of the 54 battalions that were there, three of them were Special Forces. Then they were not even known as Special Forces. They were PARA Commando battalions, 1 PARA Commando, 9 PARA commando and 10 PARA Commando. It is there for the first time that the Special Forces was created. Instead of calling it PARA Commando Cell, it was called Special Forces Cell and if I am right, I think Col Nanavati was the first OC of that cell and later on then Col Sukhi Mann came in. And it is at that time that we decided that we shall differentiate them from the other battalions because there were other PARA battalions in the force. One of those 50 odd battalions, normal battalions were called 5 PARA; and perhaps some others. So, to make sure that there is no confusion, we decided to call them Special Forces. That is the genesis of the Special Forces of the Indian Army. Their performance there, one does not praise oneself, but I was very impressed by many speakers here who were so much conversant with the great achievements of the Special Forces of our friendly foreign countries and perhaps about some not so friendly countries, not present here.

I think, to begin with, I would like to mention that there is no reason why we need, all the time to be averse to mentioning our PARA Commandos' achievements if we are looking forward for their future concepts. I will only mention one each of the PARA Commandos in Sri Lanka when I was there. Since I was there all the time, so I suppose those are the ones. Ist PARA Commando, which is responsible for a major action in which they captured certain documents, certain cassettes. It was first time told us that an Indian member of parliament had not defected but had gone over to Sri Lanka and was operating and mingling with the LTTE and also was giving the lectures against the Indian state. The commanding officer of the battalion, was Col Hardev Lidder. He was Commanding 9 PARA Commando. It happened just East of Vavuniya.

The second was another action where there was an apprehension of a special messenger of LTTE, who was carrying a letter which was a bomb. In other words it was some secret dealings with some people in India. He was nabbed and when the letter was opened, it was important enough for the Indian High Commissioner then in Sri Lanka and for me, to fly to Delhi and it was opened and presented to the then Prime Minister. That was the action of 1st PARA Commando. Then there was a situation there in which the President of Sri Lanka, the then newly elected one, went renegade as far as the India was concerned. And he threatened to throw out every one of the IPKF or whatever, but more than that he threatened our diplomatic staff and High Commissioner in Colombo. In fact he said that he could take no more responsibility for the protection of the Indian mission. So the question was whether we withdraw our mission from there. In fact I was called up to Delhi and hauled up and asked the question by the Prime Minister himself and all the ministers present as to what should be done. And a very clear decision was taken, the Indian flag flies there on Indian territory and the mission should be defended and protected. And we actually flew them in helicopters and later on we got them ready to be able to rappel in if necessary to protect the Indian High Commission. For those conversant with Colombo, it is just next door to the British Council actually. And it is very much built up in fairly crowded areas. They manned them, there was crowd outside the High Commission, I told them I will have to evacuate if necessary. He said alright but then I would like you to be the last man but I will come with you. I was also present there on that day. Crowds came, it was just a troop of the battalion concerned, which held firm. No one dared to cross over. It was clear message there that till the last man of that Para Commando or the Special Forces battalion is standing, they are not getting into the compound of soil of India. That happened to be the 10 Para Commando.

There are many other occasions. But I wish that officers, who know about these, do talk about them. It is sufficient to be proud of, to justify our placing the pedestal on which we do, our PARA Special Forces. Now there are certain points and since the rest finished before time, I think I can cover them. Mine is not a structured talk because these are closing remarks, and therefore they have to take into account the last speaker. So I will speak of them, do forgive me if they are not sequential.

Firstly, the ethos of a Special Forces unit very much depends on the country that it belongs to. The Special Forces units of the United States, I say plural, because I will talk about that later, they are plenty, are not designed to operate on the territory of the United States. So, therefore, the ethos is different. Similarly is that of the Federal Republic of Germany. They are only designed to operate outside the territory of that nation. However, in case of United Kingdom and France and perhaps India, we may have to operate within our own territory. So the ethos are conditioned by the country. But one thing is common, as we understand Special Forces are a component of the uniformed military of that nation. If anyone has a different definition then for that force, this is not the place to discuss it. That is outside in the Ministry of Home Affairs, as my esteemed colleague here did mention or some other department but not in the military. Once you are part of the uniform military, you do not have one freedom and that is to do what you want. It is not free for all. It cannot be no holds barred. Our uniformed military of nation fights under the Law of the Land. Thou shall not operate outside the law. For that, there are other agencies but the uniformed military does not besmirch itself by doing that. This is a debatable point in many countries, but certainly not in a democracy.

Now I was told that there was certain debate, it was sectarian shall we say? There was a book written in 1972. The name of the book was "The Best and the Brightest" by an American, David Helpstrom. That is when these Special Forces again had a re-generation after Vietnam. That book set the cat amongst the pigeons as far as this problem of the air borne forces, the Special Forces were concerned. That is where the controversies arose, they still carry on. So this is nothing new. We had discussions here today, it is nothing new. It has happened in the past and it will happen again in the future. Today, the US has perhaps, to the best of my knowledge, three. They have the Rangers, the Green Berets and the Delta Force. Delta force was the consequence of this book; basically these are the three I know of. So proliferation is not only in nuclear weapons but also in the various Special Forces. Apart from this, there are certain countries which have Special Forces, which have given the Special Forces a bad name. Certain countries in South East Asia and others have used Special Forces as hit squads. We shall talk about it a little later when I talk about little experience with which I will take liberty this time.

There was mention made by the esteemed speaker from United Kingdom, Gen Lamb that there is likely to be an apocalypse around 2020 when 40 or more states will have decayed or perhaps would become failed states. It is horrifying to know that there are so many decaying states today. I agree, but then that is largely a question of governance. When we talk of governance, it is to be addressed politically, not militarily. So I think somewhere we will have to be careful not to give ourselves in as you are prepared thereafter to go to war also and that is a decision the capital will have to take when the time comes, but can't be adlib launched in this kind of scenario.

The other point I would like to clarify is that there are Special Forces and there tends to be confusion between them and security forces. We must never let them associate in any form with our Special Forces which is honoured, which has some meaning. In this context, I may mention in China, the budget came out three days ago and you may like to note that for the internal use, the Chinese have realised now that they would not like to use the PLA and they want to use their own local security forces and the budget allocation of the local security forces is 2.3 times more than the budget allocation for the PLA. This should give an indication of how states manipulate their budget and this is a major power for addressing issues and problems. We may also have to learn something from China where within our country, the issue of committing the military against your own people vis-a-vis use of other forces.

A little bit about my own experience. We had the three battalions because they were highly trained, highly motivated and very well lead. There was a tendency of my divisional commanders; any difficult task, they would ask for a PARA Commando battalion or a team, that is about 120 odd people; they would like them to do it. A normal task which a normal battalion is supposed to do, as someone very well brought out, this is like a tendency to use a Derby winner to pull a cart. That tendency is obviously because they lack the confidence in their own ability to deliver. Perhaps that is one of the things which bite the Special Forces senior officers, that we are liable to get misused if they are handed over to field commanders. Probably, I am not sure, that is the worry that they will not be used properly. Maybe that is one of the causes why they want a Special Forces command, whatever it is. They have mentioned a very good idea, someone had mentioned about a Joint Special Forces command, whether the ultimate three people who are charged with the defence of their realm of the day, the three Chiefs of Staff accept or not, it is their wisdom and their decision. But whatever be it, whether the joint forces or whether under respective service, they will, as long as they are a component of the uniformed military, have to follow a certain chain of command. Should this suggestion not find favour and the Special Forces remain with the service concerned, I would beg to venture that don't go with an ongoing belief that your commander is off the line, and I don't mean a battalion, I mean your divisional commander, your corps-commanders, your Army commanders are incompetent enough not to know how to employ Special Forces. I think you are not being fair. So, should that happen, they have to go there, you have got to have faith in your chain of the command.

I should again make a mention of what Admiral Shekhar Sinha mentioned about the young boy, a naval marine in the Jaffna Peninsula actually two of them, a sub-lieutenant and another officer, who were given a task of scuttling the boats on which the LTTE, who were now being driven back, trying to escape, across the lagoon to the main land. Our worry was if they escaped, then they would be inflicting more casualty to my soldiers later. So two people were sent there and what happened was that the rest of them were ambushed, but the two were able to get away. So they decided to lie doggo there. They burnt the boats, but they couldn't get away because they were caught between the LTTE and the lagoon. And I can now understand why it is that the Admiral said that their equipment must be waterproof, for this young officer's radio set was not. He had jumped into the water to hide and they were out of communication with us. Well, the purpose was achieved, on the third day we were able to rescue him from there when we linked up our forces and he had done a magnificent job for which, I am not sure, whether he got the Vir Chakra or Mahavir Chakra. For one of two awards was immediately recommended and awarded to him. So this was that least to be said and I am only talking about the Army Special Forces. I think Navy has also achieved the task which must be recognised.

The final point to end this meeting: Use of the military in your own country. Gentlemen, 9/11 was the worst attack the US ever had on their soil. It shook them. The world was with them. The United States did not activate their military. Not even that, even the National Guard was not called out. The aircraft flying in the air was part of the NORAD defence which was there. So, countries with high democratic values tend to use less of their military for such tasks. They have other forces so this may be kept in mind because a time is now coming that there will be increasing questioning of actions, with live reporting and I do not think any man in uniform wants to get in any way entangled in a domestic situation of that kind. Having said that, I think we have all learnt a lot. I also hope that our honoured visitors from abroad have also picked up something worthwhile from us. And at the end I have to thank apart from the CENJOWS faculty, and the staff of CENJOWS, our joint sponsors, SP Guide Publications, for having made this event possible and I have no doubt that we shall be able to conduct similar get-togethers in times to come.

www.ingramcontent.com/pod-product-compliance
Lightning Source LLC
Chambersburg PA
CBHW060839100426
42814CB00016B/422/J